BECOME A LEADER
OF LEADERS

BECOME A LEADER OF LEADERS

Raise Student Achievement

Mary Ellen Freeley and Diane Scricca

ROWMAN & LITTLEFIELD
Lanham • Boulder • New York • London

Published by Rowman & Littlefield
A wholly owned subsidiary of The Rowman & Littlefield Publishing Group, Inc.
4501 Forbes Boulevard, Suite 200, Lanham, Maryland 20706
www.rowman.com

Unit A, Whitacre Mews, 26-34 Stannary Street, London SE11 4AB

British Library Cataloguing in Publication Information Available

Library of Congress Cataloging-in-Publication Data Available

ISBN 978-1-4758-0137-8 (cloth : alk. paper) — ISBN 978-1-4758-0138-5 (pbk:
alk. paper) — ISBN 978-1-4758-0139-2 (electronic)

∞™ The paper used in this publication meets the minimum requirements
of American National Standard for Information Sciences—Permanence of
Paper for Printed Library Materials, ANSI/NISO Z39.48-1992.

Printed in the United States of America

CONTENTS

FOREWORD

Schools do not stumble into excellence; they are led there by people who know what they're doing.

That seems almost so obvious as not to need stating, and yet the field of education has been slow to understand and organize itself around that fact.

Perhaps that inertia should not be surprising. After all, it took the field a very long time to acknowledge what parents and students always knew—that excellent classrooms are led by excellent teachers.

But it is long past time to understand that classroom teachers are not enough to make an excellent school. In fact, the traditional way of organizing schools around the practice of teachers working alone in their classrooms has predictable results: some students learn a lot, some learn very little, and most muddle through mediocrity.

The reason these results are predictable is that it is virtually impossible for individual teachers—even excellent ones—to know all they need to about their subjects, their students, and their pedagogy to help all their students learn all they need to learn.

The only way to meet the academic needs of all students is through close professional collaboration among all the staff of a school building—and sometimes across school buildings—to bring to bear multiple perspectives and expertise.

To organize that level of collaboration and muster whatever specialized resources their students and teachers need requires school leaders who understand instruction, know how to develop the capacity of staff members, and have the confidence to distribute leadership among others.

All of this is well established in the research literature, which this book lays out in its early pages. But we are left with the inescapable next chain of logic: If we want excellent schools and we know that excellent schools need excellent leaders, then we must ensure that all principals are excellent.

That is a bit of a daunting task. Right now, despite a great deal of work focused on instructional leadership in the last couple of decades, the principal corps as a whole can't be considered ready to organize instruction in ways that ensure high levels of academic achievement among all their students. Indeed, many current principals were trained as—and are still expected to be—middle managers who enforce district dictates while managing building operations.

The logical conclusion, then, is that the task of organizing the work of education around the central role of the school leader lies with those who recruit, hire, assign, support, and evaluate principals.

It is to these people—superintendents, district superintendents, regional superintendents, and other principal supervisors—that this book is directed.

This book argues that they, too, need to be instructional leaders, developing the capacity of the principals they supervise. Just as teachers need school leaders to help them surpass what is possible working in isolation, school leaders themselves need help to manage time and resources in service of instruction.

But we are in somewhat uncharted territory here. No solid research base exists to guide these efforts. Within a few years we may have at least the beginnings of districts around the country engage in re-thinking the role of principal supervisors. But until those results are in we must rely on the craft knowledge of highly accomplished educators who have themselves led academic improvement.

Which is where this book comes in.

My connection to the authors is through Diane Scricca, whose school I visited a few years after she had left the district. She had spent thirteen years as principal at Elmont Memorial High School in Nassau County, New York, and the culture she had established as principal was still visible when I first visited, as it is many years later—thanks to the leadership of John Capozzi, whom she hired as a teacher and helped develop as a leader. By the time I tracked Diane down she was serving as superintendent in Eastern Long Island and, as she moved on to academia, I have consulted her frequently about my own work on school leadership. She participated in the study Christina Theokas and I conducted on leadership in our book *Getting It Done: Leading Academic Success in Unexpected Schools* and helped shape our view of the principalship.

Diane frequently refers to Elmont as the love of her life—it is a large, comprehensive high school where most of the students are African American and about one-third meet the requirements for free and reduced-price meals. When Diane arrived it was a typical school with large achievement gaps. By the time she left it was outperforming most high schools in New York on almost every measure, and it continues to do so—its graduation rates have been in the high 90 percentile for more than a decade; its students enroll in college at high rates; its Regents exam results are good when not exemplary; and its achievement gaps are small when not non-existent.

Elmont has provided thousands of young people with a solid base upon which to pursue their futures and is an example of what can happen when schools have leaders who know—through a combination of good research and craft knowledge—how to run schools.

But no one should be lulled into complacency—successful schools are not perpetual motion machines that can simply be set up and expected to run forever. They require continual good leadership by people who themselves continually learn and grow.

And that means that district leaders need to understand the role principals play and how to provide the appropriate support. District leaders, in other words, also need to support and lead instruction.

It should be said that many successful school leaders are happy if their districts leave them alone. This is analogous to the fact that many successful teachers hope that their principals don't interfere with them. It is understandable, but the consequence of that isolated practice is that many districts—and schools—have what are called "islands of excellence" but cannot claim overall success.

If districts as a whole are going to be successful, district leaders must support instruction in ways that develop and share expertise through close collaboration. For district officials facing the task of organizing and supporting such work, this book provides an important starting point.

How should they begin thinking about the complicated task before them? What data should they look at to understand the situation of their principals? What goals should they set and what questions should they ask? How should they spend their time? And—not least important—what can they stop asking of principals? Which reports, meetings, and conversations take up time that could be spent in better ways?

These questions, which emerge from both research on leadership and the deep knowledge of the authors, can help begin the process of moving the field forward.

It may be long past time that the field organized itself around the importance of school leadership, but the urgency hasn't lessened one whit. There's a lot of work to do, and this book lays out some of the first steps.

–Karen Chenoweth

ACKNOWLEDGMENTS

There are many people who have contributed to my growth as a school leader over the years. It would be impossible to name and thank each one, but a few must be mentioned here. First, thanks to Dr. James Tolle, who encouraged me to pursue my administrative career and gave me the opportunity to serve as an elementary principal and then as district supervisor for curriculum, instruction, and personnel in the Malverne School District on Long Island. Second, thanks to Dr. Albert Inserra, who created a true leadership team in the Carle Place School District and supported my growth as assistant superintendent for curriculum and instruction, which paved the way for my successful twelve years as superintendent of schools.

Thanks to my assistant superintendent friends in NADCO for taking the leadership journey with me. My wonderful superintendent colleagues in Nassau County and NYSCOSS were amazing mentors as I learned more and more about school leadership—thanks to them for their support, advice, and encouragement! Finally, I am truly grateful to all the school leaders I had the pleasure of working with during my years on the ASCD Board of Directors and then as ASCD president—they broadened my understanding of school leadership from the local, national, and international levels. I am truly indebted to them for allowing me to become a leader among leaders! All of the above people and experiences have facilitated and informed my understanding and practice of school leadership and therefore influenced the writing of this book—I am most grateful!

— Mary Ellen Freeley

Becoming a leader of leaders has been a forty-year journey. I have been mentored, at every step of the educational ladder, from teacher through superintendent, by the best and the brightest. Bernard Ludwig, who was my first chairperson, taught me how a lesson plans, thereby maximizing and implementing quality instruction. He spent countless hours helping me become an effective teacher. Eileen Petruzillo, who promoted me to assistant principal, invested in me by providing direct, ongoing, and individualized supervision, ensuring that I become a supervisor that helped and supported teachers. Gerard Connors, who was my mentor as a new junior-senior high school principal, challenged me to become the best I could be through daily lessons in instructional supervision, using data to inform decisions, altering my leadership style to each teacher's individual needs, and steering me through the political waters.

I have been most fortunate in my career. There have been many other professionals who taught me lessons that I hope I learned well. The overarching quality that all of these professionals possessed, however, was the ability to teach; to teach teachers, to teach leaders. In some way, their thoughts, words, and deeds are represented on the pages of this book. I thank them all for their continued support and inspiration.

— Diane B. Scricca

LEADERSHIP

Essential to Continuous School Improvement

There is nothing more difficult to take in hand, more perilous to conduct, or more uncertain in its success, than to take the lead in the introduction of a new order of things

—Machiavelli

TENOR OF THE TIMES

Pick up any newspaper, read a political platform, listen to a national radio broadcast, or attend a local civic association meeting, and the topic will be repeated: schools are failing; they need to be reformed. Years ago, *Sputnik* was the impetus for strengthening school performance. Now, and rightly so, American students' poor performance on internationally scaled tests are dismally below their counterparts from various countries and serve as the present-day *Sputnik*.

American students, previously regarded as workers with creative, problem-solving minds, are not competitive in the global marketplace. Whether it is in mathematics, language arts, or science, today's pupils lag behind the greater worldwide community.

Everyone, educators and non-educators alike, is jumping into the arena of school reform. Race to the Top has pushed an agenda that has politicized the education field more than ever before. As a result, legislators are passing laws to regulate and improve American schools. As the baby is thrown out with the bathwater, new teacher/principal evaluation systems are being negotiated among state governments, unions, and state education departments with minimum input from practitioners and without proven research.

Districts cannot make weak principals succeed, but we have seen too many districts create conditions in which even good principals are likely to fail.
—Bottoms & Schmidt-Davis, 2010

Even schools that have effective evaluation systems are required to toss their appraisal structures and utilize state-mandated teacher assessment methods. School boards are creating policies to support these governmental decisions while district personnel scurry to implement these choices. There is no doubt—the political tsunami caused by America's poor student achievement results has caused a governmental response that has removed decision making from the hands of school leaders.

TEACHER EFFECTIVENESS IS KEY!

Clearly, raising the bar for student achievement requires that all professional educators attain a higher level of instructional understanding than they currently possess. They need knowledge of experimental educational research, and the ability to understand what contributes to the implementation of effective pedagogy (Marzano, Pickering, & Pollack, 2001; Stronge, 2002).

Wright, Horn, and Sanders (1997) found that there was no doubt that teachers are essential in this quest. Indeed, these researchers and others have discovered that teachers affect student achievement more than any other single variable.

As this research came to light, teacher competence became the focus of the federal and state governments' agenda. Simultaneously, districts were still scrambling to meet No Child Left Behind (NCLB, 2002) mandates by implementing solutions that would improve curriculum, teaching, and, ultimately, student achievement. New York State, for example, has embarked on a rather cumbersome accountability journey, including an untested teacher evaluation system. Unfortunately, there is no definable research to support its outcomes, nor is there an effective mechanism for the removal of incompetent teachers.

THE GOOD NEWS

Rather than paint an ugly landscape of the American educational system, one has only to review the latest findings of Karin Chenoweth, Pedro Noguera, Doug Reeves, and a plethora of other researchers to identify the vast array of American schools that are outperforming our international competition. In Chenoweth and Theokas' book *Getting It Done!* (2011), their research identified numerous schools that are "unexpected successes."

Throughout Chenoweth and Theokas' studies, they found many common leadership characteristics and practices in each of these high-performing schools that contributed to their achievements. From instructional leadership to strong professional development programs to creating a student-centered environment, these schools had clear strengths that contributed to their students' success. However, the one driving force behind the success of these schools was a highly effective leader at the helm.

According to Chenoweth and Theokas, effective leaders:

- Are uncompromising about the direction they have set.
- Think deeply about getting the "right people on the bus."
- Develop an organization of professional practice.

LEADERSHIP: THE ENGINE THAT POWERS STUDENT LEARNING

There are no documented cases of troubled schools being turned around without the demonstrated abilities of an effective leader (Leithwood et al., 2004). Chenoweth and Theokas' research focused on this statement as they surveyed principals who led "turnaround" schools from across the country, identifying the characteristics and leadership actions contributing to their success.

These leaders influence student learning through a myriad of sustained and complex approaches in driving change through their schools. Student achievement levels are high due to the expectation that their children WILL learn and they will not be allowed to fail. Failure is just not an option.

"Leadership is second only to classroom instruction among all school-related factors that contribute to what students learn at school . . . leadership is KEY to large scale school reform." —Leithwood et al., 2004

Effective leaders consistently utilize the data to identify problems in curriculum and teaching, develop solutions to these problems, and support their teachers in implementing resolutions. First and foremost, these leaders understand that the teacher is the front line, the essential ingredient to student success, and devote most of their efforts to supporting teacher success. Leaders who influence student learning are "teachers of teachers" (Coppola, Scricca, & Connors, 2004).

Nourishing a culture of student achievement is the primary focal point for an effective leader. In this environment, every thought, word, and action, whether it be by an administrator, teacher, counselor, or parent, is for the good of the student, ensuring his or her academic success. Classroom instruction is sacrosanct in that it is treasured time, precious time—time that is valued as the only way to ensure a high level of student accomplishment.

While evidence about leadership effects on student learning can be confusing to interpret, much of the existing research actually underestimates its effects. The total (direct and indirect) effects of leadership on student learning account for about a quarter of total school effects. —Hallinger & Heck, 1996; Leithwood & Jantzi, 2000

A CULTURE OF "WE GET WHAT WE GET"

Too often faculty rooms are filled with conversations about how students used to be, complaints about parents who do not support their children, gripes about students not doing their homework, or students who are not motivated to learn. Bill Page (2002), teacher and staff developer, states that these perceptions should not make a difference to educators. Whether students are poor, homeless, non-English speaking, or from a dysfunctional family, whatever their circumstances or disposition, these are the children we get and it is our responsibility to teach them all.

Leaders of effective schools have embraced Bill Page's philosophy. They do not accept faculty room excuses as to why students do not succeed. If parents are not participating in their child's education, effective leaders create and implement solutions such as teacher-supervised homework centers, or Saturday morning support groups offering a kind of "parental guidance."

Students who might be culturally deprived are offered a rich curriculum that might include an integrated program of cultural field trips that they never before had an opportunity to experience. English language learners attending schools with effective leaders are immersed in their "new" language through a multi-sensory environment. Water fountains, doorknobs, flags, and desks all have their dual-language names proudly displayed for all to see.

Effective leaders accept their students unconditionally; they expect their teachers to embrace the same philosophy, and they create an environment that nurtures and supports this belief system.

THERE IS NO ONE WAY TO LEAD

In our everyday life, we identify and gravitate toward people who demonstrate leadership skills because they inspire us, they motivate us, and they provide us with a vision which we strive to achieve. An everyday case in point would be choosing up teams for a neighborhood sports event like baseball. The "captains" of these teams demonstrate a kind of leadership skill in order to be chosen (or self-declared). To take this further, if you are waiting to be chosen, you already know which team you want to be on—the team captained by a former winner, the captain that made you part of the "team," the captain that made you feel capable, nurtured your abilities, and celebrated your success. Certainly, Derek Jeter, the longtime captain of the New York Yankees, demonstrates the kind of leadership skills that result in achievement, inspire team performance, and garner respect.

> *Leadership is not magnetic personality, that can just as well be a glib tongue. It is not "making friends and influencing people," that is flattery. Leadership is lifting a person's vision to higher sights, the raising of a person's performance to a higher standard, the building of a personality beyond its normal limitations.*—Drucker, 1993

Theories on effective leadership abound. However, approaches to leadership are analogous to instructional approaches in a classroom. An effective teacher is one who embraces a myriad of teaching strategies. These strategies accommodate the learning styles of their students. There is no one way to teach.

Clearly, whatever the research read, similar leadership characteristics emerge. Pursley (2002), though her research was not educationally oriented, found similar outcomes to those in the educational field; effective leaders employ diverse leadership skills to reach all they supervise and lead.

Scholarly research continually focuses on the importance of instructional leadership. However, the wider body of research on leadership emphasizes effective leadership characteristics that include creating a vision with a common set of values, shaping a culture that focuses on the student, and building relationships to sustain common goals.

"If your actions inspire others to dream more, learn more, do more and become more, you are a leader."—John Quincy Adams

---

Similarly, there is no one way to lead. For example, simply put, distributed leadership theories encourage the involvement of many participants, while the transformational theory promotes the development of a vision, a view of the future that will excite and aims to convert potential followers. Theories on situational/contingency leadership tend to focus more on the behaviors the leaders should adopt given conditional factors of employee need and performance.

However, as demonstrated in national studies on school leadership, there is not one predominant theory. Effective school leaders focus on the end result, student achievement, but take different leadership paths to get there. These pathways are influenced by teachers' professional needs and abilities, community expectations, and levels of district support.

Great leaders are like great teachers. They have knowledge of myriad approaches, understand human nature, devote themselves to learning, and utilize strategies based on the needs of those they serve.

CONCLUDING THOUGHTS

- Effective leadership is essential in ensuring a high level of academic achievement for all students.
- Effective leaders nurture and support teacher growth and success in their classrooms.
- Successful leaders accept students unconditionally and find avenues to level the playing field for all!
- Just as there is no one way to teach, there is no one way to lead!

FOR REFLECTION

Based on Interstate School Leaders Licensure Consortium (ISLLC) standard 2, as a school leader what processes do you utilize to develop an effective teaching and learning environment?

2

LEADERSHIP AND LEARNING

The Need for Professional Development

Leadership and learning are indispensable to each other.

—John F. Kennedy

Vincent Romano began his teaching career at a large, demographically diverse junior-senior high school on Long Island. The school culture was one which promoted daily professional development, supporting new teachers through observation, small group workshops, lesson plan reviews, and focused professional development goals. Vincent embraced this culture.

Inspired by his department, his supervisors, and his principal, Vincent began his journey toward becoming an effective social studies teacher. New York State social studies testing told the story of his work. His students repeatedly passed state exams with a higher than average level of proficiency. But his thirst for learning was not quenched by these successes. He continually engaged in peer observations, attended workshops, and mentored newer teachers, realizing the road to excellence was neverending. Professional development was essential to implementing cutting-edge, engaging, and rigorous teaching practices.

It was not too long before he was asked to apply for a department chair position in another district. As a new chairperson, the leader of social studies for a K–12 district, Vincent approached his responsibilities in much the same manner as he had to become an excellent teacher. He realized that to become an effective leader it was essential he immerse himself in leadership learning.

He sought out his supervisor and successful peers within and outside of his district as well as connected himself with his professional organization. He focused his learning on the observation process, curriculum development, and leadership skills while continuing his growth in the mastery of pedagogical methods.

He spent countless hours with his supervisor. They analyzed lessons together, conducted joint observations so that he might learn how to utilize this process as a professional development tool for his teachers, examined diagnostic and state exam data in conjunction with curriculum, and reviewed professional development plans. He basically spent time nearly every day reviewing how problems were approached and solved.

His devotion to his new position as a leader was as intense as it had been as a new educator. He recognized that his role as a "teacher of teachers" was critical to teacher effectiveness.

Education in the twenty-first century has changed dramatically. From the art of teaching of the last century, which spoke to the "affective" teachers who could influence their students through engaging instruction based on the strength of forceful personalities, this century has focused us on the science of our teaching. Simultaneously, research has linked strong teacher professional development programs with increased teacher effectiveness.

As a result, faculty meetings turned from administrative information sessions to faculty workshops on teaching practices. Full-day staff development programs were state-mandated for faculties across the country. Intensive multi-day conferences based on teachers' pedagogical needs became part of many schools' teacher support systems.

In many states, provisions for teacher certification were connected to required professional development hours. At long last, commitment to one's own professional development emerged as an expectation in a school's culture; the effective teachers were "life-long learners."

"It takes 2.7 hours of practice per day to improve at a skill . . . and not just routine practice, you will need to invest that time wisely by engaging in deliberate practice."—Ericsson, Prietula, & Cokely (2007)

ALL LEADERS LEFT BEHIND!

As this professional learning movement for teachers took hold in schools and districts across America, the same did not hold true for our school leaders. As leaders created professional development plans for their faculties, designed individual support plans for their teachers, examined data and curriculum, and redesigned their management plans, there was still no crusade to provide the kinds of support for our school leaders that are essential to their success.

While self-motivated and more experienced leaders might have pursued professional growth activities on their own in order to hone their skills, few formal professional learning opportunities were designed exclusively for school leaders. As school leaders began to be held more accountable for student and teacher success, little thought was given to their professional needs.

The implementation of myriad state certification mandates, common core standards, directives on teacher evaluations, and legislated requirements such as bullying prevention demand that leadership be more talented and skilled. It requires a comprehensive knowledge of a wealth of educational issues and practices. Yet support for professional learning for school leaders has not emerged as a priority on national, state, or local educational agendas. Our leaders have, indeed, been left behind!

If there is a national imperative to improve our failing schools, then there is also a national imperative to strengthen the preparation of school leaders.—Wallace Foundation, June 2008

HONORING PROFESSIONAL DEVELOPMENT FOR ALL

The research is quite clear. A major responsibility of states and districts is to provide high-quality professional development for school leaders

(Bottoms & Schmidt-Davis, 2010). Yet examine any agenda for Professional Development Day in most districts across the nation and you will find numerous staff development opportunities for teachers and yet little or none for school leaders.

One can make a case that leaders need to immerse themselves in the same instructional topics we offer our teachers. As instructional leaders, we must be masters of pedagogy. How can we lead teachers without an in-depth knowledge of effective instructional practice and concomitant research?

"Leadership is not a one-time event, it's an ongoing process of growing, evolving, and developing. . . . We found in our research that those leaders that engage more in learning are more effective as leaders."—Kouzes & Posner, April 17, 2011

Though this is true and is of great value to an instructional leader, there are management, governance, and supervisory techniques that need to be honed, strengthened, and supported. Just as teachers are expected to be lifelong learners, so, too, our school leaders must be immersed in lifelong learning in a vast number of leadership and supervisory skills.

HIGH-QUALITY PROFESSIONAL DEVELOPMENT SUPPORTS HIGH-QUALITY LEADERSHIP

An investment in professional development for school leadership is a critical element in building successful school districts and schools. Leading schools in the twenty-first century is a complex, demanding task, ever changing, requiring a level of knowledge of research that was previously ignored. Yet expectation, support, and encouragement for professional development is sorely lacking in the field of school leadership.

Getting pre-service principal training right is essential. But equally important is the training and support school leaders receive after they're hired.—The Wallace Foundation, June 2012

Comparing our professional development to that of those in the medical field is useful. For example, medical doctors immerse themselves in numerous opportunities for learning, whether it is reading research as a daily activity, attending conferences, or teaching at hospitals, the medical field demands a life of professional learning. Who would go to a doctor who was not well-informed on the latest issues and research in her field? Should we not provide the same resources and expect the same intensity toward learning for our school leaders that the medical profession does for its doctors?

The medical profession expects high-quality professional development. Similarly, the state, district, and school leadership must engage, support, and understand that more effective specialized learning practices for school leaders will result in academically successful schools. Learning activities that engage in reading, experimenting with new ideas and research-based practices, or reflecting on how we lead are just a small part of this leadership process. According to Darling-Hammond et al. (2007), "New leaders who did not receive continuing professional development once they were in the field were less likely to report high levels of effective practices."

> *Districts, for their part, need to recognize that the professional develop-*
> *ment of school leaders is not just a brief moment in time that ends with*
> *graduation from a licensing program. . . . [It must] provide well-connected*
> *development opportunities that . . . extend throughout the careers of school*
> *leaders. —M. Christine DeVita, president, Wallace Foundation, 2007*

At the beginning of this chapter, we introduced you to a highly successful school leader. In a recent interview with the authors, Vincent expounded on the comprehensive support and development he received, identifying them as the key to his success. His comments mirrored the compilation of research that states leadership must be provided, supported, and nurtured with ongoing professional growth opportunities.

He began in an environment of professional development as a teacher and then as a school leader. Acknowledging that this level of care and support for his growth is a rare but powerful circumstance, he stated that his professional life was unlike those of his peers. Certainly, there is much to learn from Vincent and the school culture that supported his evolution as an effective school leader.

As the focus of school leadership changed to instructional supervision, so did the expectations for a learned principal. Research in the twenty-first century has continued to support this thinking. To buoy this changing role, clearly developed and focused professional development for school leaders is crucial to the stewardship of our schools.

CONCLUDING THOUGHTS

While the need for ongoing professional development for teachers has been recognized and programs have been developed and implemented,

- There has been little emphasis on the continued development of school leaders.
- The changing and demanding complexity of school leader positions demands that we focus our attention on their professional growth and development.
- To ensure high levels of student achievement, it is incumbent upon districts and schools to foster a culture of professional development for all, teachers and school leaders alike.

FOR REFLECTION

Based on ISLLC standard 4, as a school leader, how do you support the collegial growth of yourself, teachers, and other administrators?

EFFECTIVE SCHOOL LEADERSHIP

Everyone's Focus, Everyone's Responsibility

The vision and actions of system leaders and school board members frequently determine whether principals can be effective in leading school improvement.

—Bottoms & Schmidt-Davis, 2010

Interestingly, in a time when societal pressure for school reform and improvement is part of our daily conversation, building- and district-level leaders simply cannot utilize their strengths and abilities to move their schools forward. Often they are stymied by school board members who, through no fault of their own, lack the educational knowledge and expertise essential to making effective decisions regarding student learning. Many board members pursue personal agendas that contribute to district dysfunction or simply do not support the leader's goals and initiatives.

This is compounded by state officials, politicians, and unions that impose rules and regulations based on political schemes and popular beliefs while creating obstacles that hamper the leaders' ability to lead. So how can principals, who require the support of state and district governance to be able to provide fearless, focused school leadership, acquire support in an educational landscape riddled with agendas?

EFFECTIVE SCHOOL LEADERSHIP REQUIRES STATE SUPPORT

How does state governance impact school leadership? Too often, we have witnessed district after district fall into a pattern of dysfunction impeding a school's academic progress. For example, New York State has mandated that each school establish a shared decision-making committee and dictates who is to serve on this committee. In theory, collaboration with various constituencies can result in decisions that are understood and supported by faculty, parents, and other school groups.

However, schools are organized differently, led differently, and require different levels of support. Many times, committees with mandated participants do not have the level of expertise and required alignment with school goals to assist in the decision-making process. The result: a poorly configured, non-research-based decision thrust upon the workings of a school.

Standards for student learning, teacher certification and evaluation, student assessments, and accountability measurements, as well as other state actions, abound. State mandates trickle down to schools with little input from school leadership, turning principals into slightly more than middle managers rather than champions of the children they serve. Imagine the frustration of a school principal who has implemented a successful teacher evaluation and observation system resulting in a high level of student achievement.

Regardless of their success, they are told by the state to abandon these processes for the adopted statewide teacher evaluation system negotiated between the state's Race to the Top criteria and the state's union leaders. Though recent research informs us that states must give school leaders more autonomy to enable them to act in an entrepreneurial fashion, the converse exists.

"Plainly put, the problem is this: Districts and states are failing to create the conditions that make it possible for principals to lead school improvement effectively."—Bottoms & Schmidt-Davis, 2010

School leaders can fight city hall! . . . They must . . .

In order to garner support for effective school leadership, administrators need to join their state and local professional organizations as well as local professional learning communities to provide input to state education offices. Participating in the creation of "white papers" on state mandates, fostering relationships with state legislators to examine state practices, working with local union leaders to analyze upcoming state initiatives, and volunteering for state committees that recommend policy can be helpful in activating support for school leadership.

This can be an exhausting exercise. It can sometimes feel like a fruitless effort. Garnering the involvement of colleagues of adjoining districts in these professional ventures while developing professional relationships to address how to respond to state mandates can provide school leaders with the kind of support needed to maintain their focus.

EFFECTIVE SCHOOL LEADERSHIP REQUIRES SCHOOL BOARD SUPPORT

In most states, school boards are governing bodies that make policy and approve budgets. Yet attend any regional superintendent function and you will hear horror stories of school board members observing classes to evaluate teachers, soliciting input from union officials on issues brought forth by the superintendent, advocating and demanding friends and family for district positions, or breaching confidentiality on personnel matters. Very often, school board members forget their role as governance and policy makers and begin to assume the role of administrators. Furthermore, they forget they have only one employee, the superintendent, and begin to act as supervisors of district faculty and staff.

The school board must be involved in developing a strategic framework for school improvement, and the board must be focused on and supportive of implementation —Bottoms & Schmidt-Davis, 2010

Yet school board members who understand their role as policy makers and supporters of district leaders can provide positive, helpful guidance in their positions. In order for this to occur, they need ongoing and intensive professional development in terms of their role as school board members and their relationship to certified school leadership. Many local school board associations provide workshops and seminars that assist school board members in understanding and executing their roles.

Perceptive school superintendents offer ongoing support for their school board members by providing guidance and background knowledge to ensure that the relationships among school board members, district office administrators, and school administrators are built on trust, mutual respect, and the importance of principal governance. Yearly retreats that have specific leadership-building activities fostering positive and supportive relationships among school board members, district office administrators, and school building leaders can provide an opportunity to build that mutual respect and trust among essential leadership partners.

EFFECTIVE SCHOOL LEADERSHIP REQUIRES DISTRICT SUPPORT

In a recent interview with a highly regarded, successful high school principal, he lamented the frivolous demands that were thrust upon him from district office administrators. Staffing decisions made without his knowledge, the burden of unnecessary paperwork, the summoning to "emergency" meetings regardless of the principal's schedule, and the lack of respect for the importance of the principal's role as the leader of the building have diminished his ability to effectively run his school. He perceives himself as the instructional leader of his building and immerses himself in professional development to continually hone his supervisory skills. As a result, his building results far surpass state data. But he is frustrated. Most of the district office team have not been principals and do not understand the demands of the position. He loves his work and his school. He knows, understands, and supports his staff and students, as evidenced by the student achievement results, but is distressed with the ongoing barrage of senseless demands, lack of support, and interference from the district office. He is seeking a position in another district.

The key organizational action districts can take to support school improvement is to define the mission of the central office as supporting principals to create the educational conditions that promote the climate, organization, instruction and practices that lead to students' success.—Bottoms & Schmidt-Davis, 2010

What is the role of the district office in relation to the principalship? To serve, to support, to guide. A recent Wallace Foundation report, *Districts Matter* (2013), emphasized that "The School District profoundly shapes the destinies of its principals: how they are trained, hired, mentored, evaluated, and developed on the job. Yet until recently, many educators and policymakers overlooked the unique role districts can play to help principals shoulder their central responsibility: improving teaching and learning."

Additionally, a recent study (Bottoms & Schmidt-Davis, 2010) identified strategies districts must implement to support, nurture, and sustain effective school leaders. School districts need to systemically provide the working conditions that well-trained principals require in order to succeed by cooperatively establishing a clear focus and a strategic plan for improving student achievement.

Furthermore, the district needs to invest heavily in instructionally-related professional learning for principals and other building supervisors. Providing high quality data that links student achievement to school and classroom practices and curriculum can help guide the principal in making thoughtful, well-planned, data-based decisions that can drive a school forward.

"Central office transformation involves strengthening the authority and attendant capacity and professional practice of both central offices and schools to strengthen teaching and learning."—Honig, Lorton, & Copland, 2009.

Finally, essential to district success, district administrators should build collaborative working relationships with principals in order to empower them and build their capacity to be real players in school reform. The principals need the authority and political cover to meet the high demands of the position, especially as it relates to curriculum, instructional methods, and personnel decisions. The effectiveness of the principal is the key in building teacher effectiveness and, ultimately, in strengthening student achievement results.

THE DILEMMA: HOW CAN DISTRICT OFFICE SUPPORT PRINCIPALS IN TEACHING AND LEARNING?

Historically, district offices have served as the organizational center of a school district. Business, personnel, and curriculum offices often support the superintendency with various other services. Among those support services provided by district offices to schools are transportation, pupil personnel, and special education. Of course, these services vary depending on the size and complexities of the district.

These central office functions were designed to regulate schools, provide and garner support for school budgets from the community, authorize individual school budgets, ensure the safety and security of students, and maintain and enhance the physical plant. Yet recent research has called for district offices to intensify the support for the teaching and learning process.

Therefore, principals need ongoing instructional and supervisory support so they can access resources that will sustain and improve teacher effectiveness, create a student-centered school culture, and hire the best and the brightest teachers who possess an educational philosophy aligned with the school. The district office must support principal autonomy, which is essential to school improvement.

Shifting the focus of the district office from organizational management to instructional support requires the re-creation and reinvention of district office personnel. If the district is to provide assistance with the teaching and learning process as well as support leadership growth, there must be a level of expertise in the district office that enables it to provide these services with credibility and authenticity. Recognition by the central office that each school within a district has its own unique culture, its own set of student needs, varied levels of instructional expertise, and diversity in leadership styles requires central office personnel to vary their approaches and levels of support to schools.

> *The district—including the school board, the superintendent, key staff, and influential stakeholders in the community—must have the capacity to develop and articulate both a vision and a set of practices that send a clear message of what schools are to be about.—Bottoms & Schmidt-Davis, 2010*

DIFFERENTIATED SUPPORT FOR SCHOOL LEADERSHIP

Changing the nature of state, board, and district support of school leadership requires a change in mindset; not all school leaders need the same levels of assistance, direction, or district management. Some schools, particularly those that are effective, as evidenced by student achievement results, will only require support and resources as requested by the principal. Yet there are schools with new principals who will require mentorship in leadership, management, culture building, and the teaching and learning process. Furthermore, ineffective school leadership will require a different level of district intervention, one which does not exclude the removal of an ineffective principal.

Just as we have learned that effective teaching must be differentiated to meet the varied learning needs of our students, so, too, must the district office vary its levels of intervention and support to its principals and other school leaders. One size does not fit all. Principals and their schools require varied levels of support which should be dependent on their level of effectiveness, reflecting their skill levels in various areas of leadership, management, and instruction.

The principal's story earlier in this chapter clearly delineates how effective principals can feel unsupported and unnecessarily micromanaged. For true school reform to transpire, state education leadership, school boards, and district offices must recognize that school building leadership is the key to this reform.

"Enacting espoused shared values and having a positive attitude were identified as the most important enablers of systemic leadership, whereas micromanagement and difficult people were the major restraints."
—Souba, 2006

CONCLUDING THOUGHTS

In order to strengthen school leadership, all facets of the school community must embrace their common responsibility.

- School leaders need multi-level support with the political cover they need to accomplish their goals.
- Supporting entities must understand their roles, understand the school leaders' needs, and possess a working knowledge of the teaching-learning process.
- Continuous, high-quality professional development and a network of peer support are essential to the growth of school leaders.
- Effective school leaders need to be empowered to conduct their business without district micromanagement.

FOR REFLECTION

Based on ISLLC standard 6, as a school leader, how do you maintain an open dialogue with all stakeholders, affording yourself an opportunity to benefit from a variety of ideas, values, and cultures?

4

WHO SHALL BE HIRED?

The best executive is the one who has sense enough to pick good men to do what he wants done, and self-restraint enough to keep from meddling with them while they do it.

— Theodore Roosevelt

A review of the literature by today's authors would certainly affirm Roosevelt's early position, but would expand on his thinking to be more gender inclusive in terms of executive leadership. In fact, a school can only be as effective as the quality of its staff. Poor leadership and poor teaching end in poor results. It is as simple as that!

Therefore, it stands to reason, the foundation of a successful school starts with the hiring process. Whether it is the employing of principals, other instructional leaders, or teachers, the focus must be the same: only the best will be hired. Finding, hiring, developing, and supporting an educational faculty that is truly the best is a leader's ultimate responsibility. The question then is *"Who is the best?"*

You absolutely must have the discipline not to hire until you find the right people.—Collins, 2001

A *middle school within a large suburban district needed a new princi-*
pal. The former principal of five years moved to another district and was
followed for one year by an interim principal appointment. The school
results were stagnant. The staff was quite demoralized from having two
principals in six years. The lack of student success permeated the school's
culture. Apparently, the principal who had been there for five years had
been ineffective; he was unable to make decisions, was micromanaged by
the superintendent, and did not have good interpersonal skills.

When it was time to hire a new principal, Peter, an affable person
within the district office, applied. A former dean of students before he
worked in personnel, Peter possessed a wonderful manner with people.
He made everyone feel good about themselves. The superintendent felt
he was exactly what the school needed, someone who could boost morale
and develop a working relationship with the staff! Peter was chosen as
the next principal. He hired two assistant principals and an English
chairperson who were equally charming. They were all hardworking
professionals who cared deeply about the school and the community.

After five years, the school's student achievement results dipped
lower. Peter was beloved by the community and staff but could not move
the school in the right direction. He made decisions, but they were all to
make everyone happy.

> *It is the principal, more than anyone else, who is in a position to ensure*
> *that excellent teaching and learning are part of every classroom.—Wallace*
> *Foundation, June 2012*

In the scenario above, never was the level of instructional expertise, leadership ability, prior experience, or curriculum knowledge assessed or addressed. Similarly, when the principal hired personnel for his school, he focused only on personal skills, not on the pedagogical and leadership skills that were so desperately needed in this school.

Work ethic and caring for one's professional work are certainly important leadership characteristics to possess, but unto themselves, they are not enough to change a school's culture or improve student achievement results.

> *Principal hiring takes place without a proper assessment of an applicant's*
> *training or motivation for the job.—Wallace Foundation, 2013*

Christopher Cerf, formerly New York City's deputy schools chancellor, puts it this way: "Pick the right school leader and great teachers will come and stay. Pick the wrong one and, over time, good teachers leave, mediocre ones stay, and the school gradually (or not so gradually) declines. Reversing the impact of a poor principal can take years. . . . Too often, however, school districts don't invest the requisite level of care, resources and hard work into the critical mission of recruiting and identifying school leaders. . . . Most districts have neither the capacity nor data systems to infuse rigor into the principal selection process, and so they rely on their best judgment, and sometimes even pure inertia." (Center for American Progress, 2011).

So if this is how most school systems choose their leadership, how can we change our processes to ensure the selection of effective leaders?

ENSURING THE SELECTION OF HIGH-QUALITY SCHOOL LEADERS

How we hire is as important as who we hire! Too often local politics, the lack of a focused, goal-oriented hiring process, insufficient identification of the requisite qualities and skills essential to success in the position, or disagreement among those involved in the hiring as to who should be brought in complicate a district's employment processes.

Furthermore, in many instances, candidates are brought forward for leadership positions based on who they know as opposed to what they know and what they can contribute to the success of the district. In fact, these issues cloud the process and render it an ineffective selection system. These kinds of situations result in the hiring of poorly qualified candidates who have attained leadership positions which they cannot successfully fulfill.

"Hiring is the most important job we all do. If you don't have time to hire great people, think about how much time you're going to spend working with not great people."—Lenz, April 25, 2010

So who is ultimately responsible for hiring for school positions, whether it is an assistant superintendent, principal, or teacher? Tables of organization clearly delineate positions within an organization as well as clearly define concomitant responsibilities. These documents define the location of each position within a supervisory landscape and the specific job responsibilities for each position.

Most importantly, they establish who evaluates all employees within an organization. These tables of organization were developed with a specific purpose in mind: supervisory and evaluation responsibilities.

However, this organizational tool is often ignored during the hiring process. As a result, those involved in the hiring process begin to assume responsibility across, within, and between the district's organizational structures. Hiring choices are then decided by people who might not directly supervise or evaluate the candidate.

A ROAD MAP FOR HIRING RESPONSIBILITIES

Since the table of organization delineates who directly evaluates each person within the system, it should also indicate who should be responsible for hiring for each position. Hiring a "team" for a district or school requires an in-depth knowledge of the district/school culture, its mission and vision, and the specific goals and objectives of the institution. It also requires that all administrators and teachers fully understand who their supervisors are and what their responsibilities are within the organization.

"First, build a large core of well-qualified candidates for the principalship . . . . Establish selective hiring procedures that identify the most promising future leaders and match them to the right schools."—Wallace Foundation, 2013

For example, the superintendent is the sole employee of the Board of Education. Therefore, the Board of Education hires the superintendent. To continue with this illustration, the superintendent must hire all district office personnel and principals. Principals are responsible for hiring all leadership, faculty, and support staff within their building. When hiring processes are not congruent with the table of organization, a level of dysfunction and micromanagement can and will set in.

ROLE OF COMMITTEES IN THE HIRING PROCESS

Committees do not hire. They recommend. They participate in the hiring process as part of an inclusive school culture. They are involved in reviewing all aspects of a candidate, but ultimately, the actual hiring for a position is the sole responsibility of the person who will supervise and evaluate that candidate. This is the ultimate responsibility in the area of accountability.

> *Districts commonly do not allot enough time or resources to making the appropriate match between local school/district leadership needs and candidates' demonstrated skills and abilities.—Clifford, 2012*

Committees for the hiring of principals are often utilized in school districts. Yet many committee members are unschooled in the hiring process, come with specific agendas, or have no knowledge of the level and variety of skills that are essential to success in the position. Without expertise, the selection process will result in faulty choices.

In Hoy and Tarter's (1995) work on decision making, they clearly state that effective committee decisions require that committee members possess two prerequisite qualifications: expertise in the focus of the committee's work and a personal stake in the committee's outcomes.

For example, if a committee member has a personal agenda that influences the outcome of a committee's recommendation, the outcome will be tainted and not aligned with the purpose of the committee or the purpose of the organization. Additionally, if a committee member does not have the expertise or knowledge base to ascertain if a candidate has the instructional/leadership skills essential to success in the position, the committee member will not be able to effectively contribute to the committee's outcome.

A HIRING PROCESS THAT WORKS!

In *Supportive Supervision: Becoming a Teacher of Teachers* (2004), Coppola, Scricca, and Connors present a hiring process directed by hiring goals, supported by the training of hiring committee members, and focused on hiring the best candidates. To hire the best candidate for a position, it is essential that all parties involved in the process learn how the hiring process will be conducted, receive specific and focused training on how the committee will work, delineate the precise skills critical to the position, and ultimately, provide a specific hiring plan to ensure that the process will result in identifying the best candidate for the position.

"Our students and our community deserve no less than the very best. The most dedicated, the most talented men and women. . . . However, finding them can be a very difficult task."—Coppola, Scricca, & Connors, 2004

The graphic illustration on page 32 presents an organizational process that will result in identifying and hiring the best school leaders.

CONCLUDING THOUGHTS

A school's accomplishments are directly related to the effectiveness of its professionals.

- The success of a school starts with hiring the best leader.
- The district's table of organization delineates who should do the hiring.
- Committees participate in the hiring process solely to make recommendations.
- It is essential that all parties involved in the hiring process be well trained and understand and uphold the designated procedures.

FOR REFLECTION

Based on ISLLC standard 2, as a school leader, how do you nurture and sustain a culture of collaboration, trust, learning, and high expectations among newly hired staff?

5

HIRING THE BEST SCHOOL LEADERS

Current research makes clear that the school principals play a critical role in improving student performance. Therefore the quality of education that can be delivered to students rests on a school district's ability to bring quality principals on board. . . . Enhancing recruitment, building a truly rigorous selection process and aggressively advancing the principal hiring timeline requires the right people, adequate resources and institutional determination.

—Broad Foundation, 2006

Numerous reports from the Broad and Wallace foundations have indicated that districts must create systems to help them identify and hire highly qualified leaders for their schools. Furthermore, their research delineates a variety of specific processes that ensure that a rich pool of candidates for leadership openings is secured and the best school leaders are hired. As a result of these studies and years of experience in the field, this chapter presents a hiring road map (see Figure 5.1) that outlines the steps to be taken to ensure the best principals and school leaders are hired.

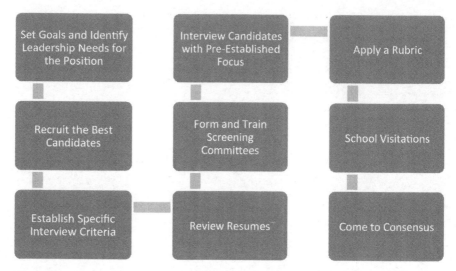

Figure 5.1.   A Road Map Leading to Hiring the Best Principals

SET GOALS AND IDENTIFY LEADERSHIP NEEDS

To hire the best person, it is essential to develop a set of hiring goals and position needs to direct the process. For example, if a district is hiring for a secondary school principal, how important is it that the candidate possess secondary school experience and how long should that experience be? Considerations related to the school population need to be clearly identified. A school that has a large Hispanic population might be best served with a bilingual principal. If a high school staff has a senior faculty with particular instructional needs in mathematics, might the school be best served with a principal with a strong background in mathematics instruction?

Many districts lack the tools and processes to create a good match between a candidate's qualifications and the needs of particular schools.—Wallace Foundation, 2013

Characteristics of the Leader

Before the hiring process begins for any school leader, or teaching position, establishing explicit criteria for those positions will ameliorate any questions as to who should be hired. These criteria should include the characteristics, both professional and personal, that are essential to successful leadership in the school. A caring, passionate listener who can inspire the staff while providing a myriad of leadership styles might be just the prescription needed for a school.

Whatever the characteristics identified as essential to success in the position, an explicit list of these vital qualities needs to be developed. Sharing with and explaining to the hiring committee why these qualities are essential for success in the position will enable the committee to make an informed recommendation.

Special Skills

Any special skills that would enhance the effectiveness of the school leader, such as second language proficiency, a deep understanding of instruction and its correlation to operative leadership, problem-solving skills, or an ability to bring together a fractured staff, should be clearly identified before the process begins. Each school presents a different culture, different staff needs, and unique student strengths and challenges. The skill set of the prospective leader should match the needs of the constituency he or she will serve.

The recruitment and selection process should be highly personalized and extensive, consider the school context and individual capabilities when making a match.—Hitt, Tucker, & Young, 2012

Background Commensurate with Position Needs

The kind of school for which we hire should dictate the educational background and experience we seek in our candidates. If hiring for an elementary school with poor literacy results, it should be established that the candidate needs extensive experience as an elementary school teacher, with specific, proven literacy expertise and achievement. Teaching certifications are established by specific grade levels, content, and specializations. So, too, should our hiring practices give great consideration to the grade-level training of our prospective leaders. Child development needs are very different in each school configuration.

Our school leaders need to be experts in the school levels they lead and the academic disciplines that will need to be strengthened.

RECRUIT THE BEST CANDIDATES

The single most important aspect of the hiring process is creating a pool of candidates that are strong applicants, possessing a wide range of diverse skills, personal qualities that will stand the test of leadership, and an in-depth understanding of the complexities of effective instruction. Not an easy task, but one that demands capturing candidates with various experience levels. Strategic recruiting, outside the traditional realm of staffing, can produce a pool of strong candidates for a school district.

School districts allocate less time and less funding to leadership position searches than private businesses or non-profit agencies, which hampers hiring committees' abilities to holistically evaluate candidates.—Hollenbeck, 1994

Traditional Advertisements

Whether in national or local papers, advertisements should not be disregarded as a means of developing a pool of candidates. This form of recruitment frequently brings in the largest number of applicants. Additionally, many regional district offices provide online advertisement services that reach a large audience of educators. However, districts need to expand these advertisements to newspapers that cater to various minority groups, such as the New York papers *Amsterdam News*, which is read predominantly by the African American community, and *El Diario*, which is read predominantly by the Spanish-speaking community. Inclusionary recruitment can bolster the candidate pool while providing the district with a more diverse group of applicants.

Leadership Academies

These academies have been developed by many districts to groom future leaders. Just as a student-teacher program can produce a strong pool of candidates for teaching positions, a district leadership academy can actively develop and ultimately produce future school and district leaders. These leadership academies may be offered with a local university, professional organization, and/or within the district itself.

"There needs to be a coordinated, strategic approach within school systems and schools for attracting and retaining principals and for succession planning for educational leadership in the future."—Chapman, 2005

Utilizing successful district and school leaders to serve as workshop presenters and mentors within the academy can result in generating a "farm system" similar to that in baseball for the leadership needs of the district. Academy participants will receive ongoing training, mentoring, and experiences that can help a district decide if they have the skill set to be successful leaders in the district.

Professional Networks

Whether national, local, or informal, groups of professional peers should serve as a source for potential candidates. Notification through publications, listservs, or personal phone calls can expand your candidate pool beyond traditional recruitment efforts.

"Be strategic about recruiting. Develop and maintain professional networks outside the organization that may serve as sources for candidates or recommendation of candidates and notify the people in your network when vacancies arise."—Clifford, 2012

Adjunct Professors In Local Universities

These positions are often sought by local school administrators. As a college instructor, it is essential to read the latest research, create syllabi, and keep abreast of the latest in technology and instruction.

This, of course, strengthens the leader's skills and abilities. However, another by-product of this activity is access to a pool of future leaders. Often, while teaching a class of professionals, the instructor identifies those who shine above the others, demonstrating a strong work ethic, superb problem-solving skills, and other leadership characteristics. This is an excellent opportunity to identify those particular professionals that will fit into the future leadership of a district.

Does Anyone Have a Friend?

A strong, highly effective district usually has a strong group of effective leaders and teachers. These faculty and leaders can serve as district recruiters by identifying other educators they know who could possibly fill the open position. Postings within the district, while encouraging present employees to actively seek applicants, may result in a richer pool of candidates.

ESTABLISH SPECIFIC INTERVIEW CRITERIA

Often, when positions are advertised, a barrage of inquiring phone calls and visits to district office personnel with a "friend's" resume in hand is standard. Board members, fellow professionals, union officials, and former colleagues come knocking on the door requesting interviews. These "courtesy" interviews can enhance your candidate pool if the same criteria established for all candidates are applied to the courtesy pool. The specific job qualifications, essential work experiences, certifications, and professional characteristics identified by the district as essential for successful candidacy are expected for courtesy interviews.

READING RESUMES

Crucial to creating a pool of highly qualified candidates is reading resumes with focus, knowledge, objectivity, and consistency. An application of standard criteria to all resumes is essential in weeding out poorly skilled candidates while identifying those whose skills and background best match the needs of the position.

Additionally, resume reading requires focusing on the following specific details.

- Examine the resume's organization, neatness, and grammar, which are indicators of a person's attention to detail and administrative tasks.
- Review years of employment thoroughly. Are there any gaps of employment that need to be explained? Has the candidate moved from position to position frequently (less than three years)? Have leadership positions been downgraded (returned to an assistant principal position from a principal position)?
- Had tenure been denied or the candidate's position changed prior to the awarding of tenure?
- Does the resume indicate a desire to lead? Does the candidate have experience teaching in college, being a committee chair, making presentations at national or state conferences, holding an office in a professional organization?
- Beware the attachments! Did the candidate respond to the advertisement as indicated or did he or she inundate you with portfolios and attachments that were never requested?
- In reviewing the employment history, look for the prior supervisors of the candidate. If you know them, call them.
- Examine the references in terms of the position they hold and their relationship to the candidate. Be sure they are contacted before the candidate is offered the position.

FORMING AND TRAINING SCREENING COMMITTEES

A screening committee needs to include those who are aligned with the goals of the school and have knowledge about the school and its culture, its students and their needs, and the faculty and their strengths and weaknesses. The committee should include administrators and supervisors from the school and a cross section of teachers and support staff.

Though there are some districts that include board members, parents, and students in the committee process, their lack of expertise and knowledge can allow personal agendas, inexperience, or outside influences to taint the committee process. Professionals need to hire professionals. When training a screening committee, its purpose must be made clear: the committee recommends. The supervisor of the position makes the actual selection.

"Committee members commonly make decisions about candidates within the first three minutes of an interview and base these decisions upon personal attraction, candidate reputation, or candidate similarities to the search committee member. . . . The hiring process should be methodical in surfacing these initial reactions and helping committee members . . . make a well-informed decision."—Clifford, 2012

INTERVIEWING CANDIDATES WITH PRE-ESTABLISHED FOCUS

The committee needs to be clear on the mission and culture of the school, school goals, data indicators, and specific skills essential for the candidate to be effective. Common focus will result in a common decision. Prior to the interview, questions related to all these criteria need to be formulated and assigned to each committee member. It is most important that a similar set of questions be asked to each candidate, enabling the committee to compare and contrast the skill set of each applicant.

Dos and Don'ts for Interviewing Candidates

- Do stick to a time schedule
- Don't go beyond thirty minutes
- Do put candidates at ease
- Don't forget copies of resumes for all committee members
- Do ask similar questions of all candidates
- Don't forget to ask follow-up questions

- Do have all committee members ask questions
- Don't ask trick questions
- Do give verbal feedback

—Coppola, Scricca, & Connors, 2004

Be sure to review housekeeping issues with the committee. How many hours will be spent interviewing? How long will each interview last? Will there be discussion about each candidate between each interview or at the end? Who will welcome the candidate and be the chair of the committee that will hold everyone accountable to the interviewing criteria that has been established? When will the candidates learn of the result of the committee?

UTILIZING A RUBRIC OR RATING SCALE

To maintain objectivity, an instrument, whether it be a rubric or rating scale, should be applied for each candidate's interview. Committee members should be familiar with the instrument prior to the interviews, be required to gather specific evidence from the candidate's conversation, and base their recommendations on the data gathered through the instrument. Time should be allotted between each interview for members to use the instrument to rate each candidate.

VISIT THE FINAL CANDIDATES' PRESENT SCHOOL AND POSSIBLE FUTURE SCHOOL

Two visits! If our commitment to find the best match for the position is genuine then two visits should occur. Select members of the committee should visit the candidate's present school to meet with supervisors and those the candidate supervises. Both formal and informal conversations with stakeholders can concretize the committee's evaluation from the interviews or provoke further questions about the candidacy, requiring additional inquiry.

Conversely, the final candidates should visit the school where the position is being filled. Give the candidates the task of spending the day in the school, in any fashion they deem appropriate, that would further their knowledge regarding the culture and needs of the school. This could be followed by a second interview asking the candidates why they chose to interview the stakeholders they did, to discuss their findings from their conversations and data reviews, and to create a plan of action to strengthen school performance.

> *A one-day, on-site visit by the finalist's candidates to the school can help search committee members and candidates make decisions about the quality of the match.—Clifford, 2012*

COMING TO CONSENSUS

Utilizing the rubric and data collected from school visits, the committee chair should ask each member to rate the candidates and choose the best candidate. If position criteria are well-defined, the committee should easily come to consensus as to who the best candidates for the position are.

CONCLUDING THOUGHTS

A process is necessary in order to hire the best school leaders.

- A hiring system must be created, disseminated, and rigorously adhered to for qualified school leaders to be identified and selected.
- Those involved in selecting school leaders must understand the culture, needs, and direction of the school.
- Maintaining objectivity is paramount in each phase of the hiring process.

FOR REFLECTION

Based on ISLLC standard 3, as a school leader, how do you ensure the hiring process will produce top-quality candidates who will be able to create and sustain a safe, efficient, and effective learning environment for all students?

6

CREATING INSTRUCTIONAL LEADERS

> Research in educational administration suggests in particular that principals that focus their efforts on creating a school environment conducive to teaching and learning—so-called instructional leadership—are most likely to facilitate school improvement.
>
> —Robinson, Lloyd, & Rowe, 2008

In reviewing recent literature, there is no uncertainty: effective school leadership is second only to teacher effectiveness as the foundation of school success and improvement. As one reads the volume of research on this subject, the term "instructional leadership" becomes the mantra of principal effectiveness. To be a strong, productive principal, first and foremost, one must be an instructional leader.

WHAT IS INSTRUCTIONAL LEADERSHIP?

Most agree, instructional leaders are passionately immersed in the teaching and learning process. Whether it be working directly with teachers on the implementation of pedagogical strategies or identifying teacher professional development needs, instructional leaders recognize and support educational practices that affect student achievement.

If our educational system is to deliver on the promise of high standards for all students, educational leadership must strive to create conditions for high quality instruction in every classroom. The historical paradigm—in which instruction is solely the purview of the teacher, to the exclusion of administrators, superintendents and policy makers—is an obstacle to reaching our academic goals for children.—Elmore, 2004

However, instructional leadership requires administrators to have a broader perspective on what affects instruction in schools. This should include:

- Creating a school vision that drives the school culture.
- Hiring the best faculty.
- Ensuring instructional practices are based on data analysis and recent pedagogical research.
- Focusing on the alignment of curriculum, instruction, and, ultimately, assessment.
- Creating a school environment that necessitates, yet, supports continuous professional learning for all educators.

WHO SHALL LEAD?

Instructional leadership has different structures in each school environment. These structures are dependent on the size, intricacies, and curriculum variations in a school. For example, the principal of a small elementary school with fifteen teachers on faculty can become an expert in the curriculum, literacy, and mathematical standards students must master before entering middle school.

In contrast, on the secondary school level, the demands of a multi-disciplinary, college- and career-ready curriculum coupled with the large number of faculty in a high school change the dynamics of what instructional leadership looks like. Therefore, secondary school leaders need to develop an organizational approach to instructional leadership.

This might include departmental chairpersons, instructional assistant principals, or other curriculum leaders that work in conjunction with the principal to maintain the focus and support of the teaching and learning process. Teachers need instructional support. An organizational design that sustains ongoing professional growth models is different dependent on school size, student academic level, and school configuration.

LEADERSHIP CULTURE MUST KEEP THE FOCUS ON INSTRUCTION

Janet opens the high school year by meeting with her faculty. She reviews school rules. Students may not wear hats in school or carry cell phones. Cutting and lateness policies are reviewed, as well as board policies on the code of conduct. If students fight, they will be suspended. Teachers must follow up with parent phone calls, send discipline referrals to deans, and be consistent in their approach to the application of policies. Professional development on the practices of "assertive discipline" will continue for the third year.

Her first meeting with her students mirrors the faculty meeting. There will be a zero tolerance policy on breaches of the school code of conduct. She informs her students that learning cannot take place in an undisciplined environment. Behavior is tantamount to student success. She relays her disappointment in the student achievement data from last year's graduating class and communicates to her students that this must improve.

She is well-respected by parents, teachers, and students. The school is safe.

Unfortunately, this is a frequent scenario in the underperforming schools that are identified in every state by poor assessment results. Frequently, these leaders are considered "successful" because the building is under control. However, with an emphasis on discipline rather than instruction, a culture is created that is devoid of the impact of effective teaching and learning on student achievement and discipline.

Effective principals ensure that their schools allow both adults and children to put learning at the center of their daily activities. Such a "healthy school environment," as Vanderbilt researchers call it, is characterized by basics like safety and orderliness as well as less tangible qualities such as a "supportive, responsive attitude" toward the children and a sense by teachers that they are part of a community of professionals focused on good instruction.—Wallace Foundation, January 2012

A successful school is driven by a highly instructional-focused leadership culture. Contrary to the above anecdote, an instructional leader embraces a philosophy: all school success is directly related to classroom instruction. The stronger and more effective the instruction, the more successful student achievement results are.

No matter the socioeconomic environment students are from, schools with robust instructional programs can overcome all obstacles to learning. One only has to review the work of Karin Chenoweth and The Education Trust to know that leadership and teachers do make a difference in any school!

"With accountability standards creating more public scrutiny than ever before, educational leaders must focus their efforts on instruction if they are to thrive and survive in current conditions."—Elmore, 2004

Instructional leadership encompasses certain cultural elements that demonstrate the principal's primary focus in his/her hierarchy of responsibilities in the teaching and learning process. It includes the following four elements:

- Academic success for all!
- Schoolwide culture of learning.
- Data analysis drives programmatic and instructional decisions.
- Educational research and global demands impact instruction choices.

Academic Success for All!

In order for our students to compete in a global economy, a solid educational foundation is essential to ensure that they are successful. This drives a leadership culture to have high expectations for all students, including those who arrive from low socioeconomic households, need special education services, and are English language learners. It demands that all faculty act on this belief in all instructional decisions and approaches.

Leadership cultures that advocate, support, and even mandate a rigorous curriculum for all make this abundantly clear to all constituents in a school, not just faculty. Students, parents, and the local community understand the school is a place where each child will be expected to excel, not just meet their potential.

A leadership culture of high student expectations is one that gives access and equity to all students. This is a culture that ensures every child will read by seven years old: no gaps, no excuses. This is a culture that doesn't open accelerated classes for a select few but expects all students to be engaged in a competitive academic environment. This is a culture where college is a natural step in each student's educational journey. This is a culture where the unending remediation road is not evident, since extra time with a rigorous curriculum supplants remediation. This is a culture where the belief in every child's capacity to learn, though differently, is addressed in every classroom, every day!

In a culture of high expectations, the role of the principal is to remove barriers to success. An effective principal understands the importance of high expectations and is committed to working collaboratively with their staff to make needed changes. He or she is an advocate for changing instruction. They lead the conversation with their staff. Most of all, they are comfortable challenging long-standing beliefs and norms about schooling. They focus intently on student learning and make every program, policy, and practice at their school convey to students that they are expected to achieve at very high levels and that they will be successful.—Education Partnerships, Inc., 2013

Schoolwide Culture of Learning

Mr. King, the principal of an elementary school, meets a teacher in the hallway who he knows is grappling with an instructional approach for a specific math topic that her students are having difficulty with. He informs her that he found an article in a math journal that addresses the issues and recommends that after she reads it, she come to his office. He would love to discuss her reaction to the article.

The next day, the teacher arrives at his office with three other teachers who all read the journal article. They spend several hours discussing the article and its recommended approaches, and they spend time collaboratively designing two units to integrate these suggestions.

In successful schools, learning goes beyond the classroom. The culture of learning permeates every aspect of school life. Teachers engage with each other and with administrators as a team, approaching classroom instruction together. This instructional team examines their practices, refines curriculum, reviews student achievement data, reads the latest research, and shares successes. As a result, they develop instructional approaches that meet the needs of all children. In a school that possesses a culture of learning, these kinds of professional dialogues and activities are a daily occurrence.

The 1996 ISLLC standards call for the principal to be "an educational leader who promotes the success of all students by advocating, nurturing, and sustaining a school culture and instructional program conducive to student learning and staff professional growth."

Data Analysis Drives Programmatic and Instructional Decisions

Using data to inform instruction has become the mantra of present-day educational practice. However, our most successful schools have engaged in this practice since the early 1960s. In states and districts such as New York, where Regents examinations have been in existence since 1864, the use of data to determine student strengths and weaknesses would frequently indicate the need for curriculum revisions and changes in classroom instruction.

Subsequently, the use of student data has expanded and grown to include more variables than ever before. For example, the use of instructional, demographic, programmatic, and anecdotal data has become an ongoing process rather than a mid- or end-of-year activity. The use of this data is essential to close achievement gaps while preparing our students for a globally competitive world.

Effective school leaders, role models in data analysis, utilize data daily, as it is an integral part of the school improvement process. Schools that utilize data to inform decisions at every level use it as a continuous strategy in the instructional process. These schools not only examine state assessment data, but actively engage with data for every class assignment, quiz, and classroom assessment.

Grade-level teams are data teams that realize it is their curriculum and instructional decisions that impact student achievement results. They understand that classroom practices are the cause and the data are the effect.

"Principals and other school leaders should spend the majority of their time on classroom instructional activities such as evaluating student work with teachers, providing feedback on assessments, planning and providing professional development, reviewing achievement data, and studying building-level data on teaching practices."—Reeves, 2002

Educational Research and Global Demands Impact Instructional Choices

Peter Senge stated that reflection and inquiry (the use of empirical evidence) are not practiced much. The art of teaching has become the science of teaching. The research on the brain, the teaching/learning process, teacher effectiveness and its impact on student achievement, or almost any other school-related topic has considerably improved and increased over the past thirty years.

Combine this kind of research with the global demands of the job market. A school leader must know how to make program decisions and curriculum recommendations, implement new faculty, or simply create classrooms that reflect worldwide technology. The leader's challenge is how this research is utilized in making decisions at the district and school level.

ARE YOU AN INSTRUCTIONAL LEADER?

In order for you to consider whether you are an instructional leader we must first identify the leadership practices that are considered instructional. These practices might include:

- Observing teachers, other faculty, and school administrators.
- Engaging in curriculum development and alignment.

- Reviewing student assessment data to identify student, teacher, and program strengths and weaknesses.
- Designing professional development plans based on student and teacher needs.
- Being a *teacher of teachers*.

Recent research has expanded conventional instructional leadership practices to include organizational management focused on instructional improvement. As indicated at the beginning of this chapter, instructional leadership differs dependent upon the size and level of the school. Therefore, where expertise in subjects is more intense, as at the secondary level, the principal's ability to coordinate instructional improvement through a variety of school leadership models is key in providing instructional support and evaluation.

If you spoke to principals or other school administrators and asked them if they were instructional leaders, certainly they would say, "Yes! It is the most important work I do!" However, how can school leaders be sure that they are spending a significant part of their day on instructional matters?

Ask yourself whether you have engaged in the following **daily** activities:

- How much time did I spend in classrooms?
- Have I attended grade-level meetings, department meetings, or other instructional focus groups?
- How many observations did I conduct today, this week, this month, this year?
- Have I identified those teachers who need more assistance and provided the support essential to their success?
- What kinds of instructional professional development activities have I participated in? My faculty? And do these activities reflect the professional needs of those involved?
- Did I read professional journals?
- Am I providing and engaging in opportunities for teachers to improve their instructional practices?

CONCLUDING THOUGHTS

Effective school leaders spend a significant portion of their day on instructional matters.

Instructional leadership's primary focus is on the teaching and learning process.

- There are specific leadership practices that are considered instructional.
- Instructional leadership encompasses certain cultural elements.
- Organization management must also be focused on instructional improvement.

FOR REFLECTION

Based on ISLCC standard 3, as a school leader, how do you ensure that teacher and organizational time is focused to support quality instruction and student learning?

7

CLASSROOM OBSERVATIONS

The Foundation of Professional Development

[There is] a call on leaders to attend to the work of continuous improvement of instruction through the supervision process even in the face of dwindling professional development funding. The best resource for professional development is ongoing professional feedback . . . not criticism, but skilled meaningful, targeted feedback.

—Berkowicz & Myers, 2014

If you want to discover how the teachers in your school or district perceive the observation process, enter the faculty room. Ask them what the purpose of the observation process is and ask them to write down their feelings. Then leave the room.

What you will learn is that the observation process is one of the most misunderstood supervisory practices in school systems across America. Many teachers believe observations are something that the supervisors have to "get done." It is "snoopervision," as one teacher recently stated after her supervisor left the room, "The process has no impact on my professional growth." The teacher just does what "they" want to see.

Observations are primarily viewed as a way for supervisors to check to ensure that teachers are doing their job. They come in and evaluate the teacher's performance through the observation of a single lesson. Most teachers view this as a professional intrusion.

There are supervisors who enter classrooms and tell teachers either in writing or in conversation that they did a good job with one aspect of the lesson and a bad job with another. Usually, an observation report is predetermined by the supervisor without any professional discussion with the teacher. The worst scenario is the supervisor who observes the class and emails the report to the teacher for his or her signature. It is no wonder that teachers within this kind of supervisory culture think so poorly of the observation process.

With the advent of annual professional performance reviews, such as those implemented in New York State, the problem worsens. Observations are now weighted and included as part of the end-of-year evaluation, changing the form and purpose of observations. Supervisory observations now involve checking classrooms, evaluating instruction, and giving a score that is linked to a district's formula.

This is not to say that there aren't schools with effective principals that have created a school culture that supports professional growth. However, by and large, as found in a recent study (Romano, 2012), teachers' perception of observations is less than helpful in improving instruction, can be intrusive to the classroom, and is viewed as not contributing to professional growth.

WHAT IS THE TRUE PURPOSE OF CLASSROOM OBSERVATIONS?

Glickman, Hunter, and Danielson, as well as so many other educational thinkers, have clearly stated that observations, when properly conducted, can provide a rich professional development experience for teachers. The observation process, in its purest form, affords a professional forum for the supervisor and teacher to improve instructional effectiveness.

"One primary task for principals, perhaps the primary task, is to design opportunities for teachers to engage in professional learning that has an unmistakable impact on the way they teach and the way students learn."—Knight, 2011

However, too often, classroom observations are referred to as evaluations. The word evaluation in itself suggests an assessment as to whether what is being observed has worth or merit. It infers appraisal, rating, or an estimation of value. The question, therefore, is what is the purpose of classroom observations? Is it an opportunity to provide ongoing instructional support, a process that nurtures growth and ensures the creation of instructional environments that promote student learning? Or is it evaluation to simply determine whether teachers are meeting school leaders and district expectations?

The answer to this question can depend on the caliber of the professional. Professionals who do not view their own professional growth as essential to student achievement create an atmosphere where the observation can be used as an evaluative tool. However, for most teachers, the purpose of the classroom observation is:

- To provide individualized staff development to every teacher on a consistent basis.
- Through a cooperative effort, to create an environment for the sharing of ideas, experience, and expertise with continuous instructional improvement becoming the ultimate goal.
- To foster the teacher's ability to self-reflect on daily lessons and implement essential instructional decisions to improve instruction.
- To analyze teacher strengths and weaknesses to enable the supervisor to formulate departmental, school, and district-wide professional development plans.

Ultimately, to effect teacher growth through an instructional observation process, the supervisor must possess a high level of instructional expertise while exhibiting patience, sensitivity, and a genuine interest in the teacher's improvement. This can be accomplished in an atmosphere that provides clear and consistent support as well as continuity in the supervision process.

There is no question that how a supervisor implements the observation process creates teachers' perceptions of the purpose of the process. If we want to develop school cultures that demonstrate a healthy respect for instruction, where teachers are supported, where instruction is the highest priority for all professionals, then the implementation of the observation process must be viewed as the foundation of all professional development.

CREATING SUPERVISORY OBSERVATION GUIDELINES SUPPORTING INSTRUCTIONAL GROWTH

As was discussed at the beginning of the chapter, how a faculty views the observation process lies primarily in how supervisors administer the process. Clearly, the supervisor must demonstrate daily that the improvement and support of the instructional program is the most important task in the hierarchy of their responsibilities.

"Giving feedback effectively to teachers can be among the most important contributions a principal can make to improving the quality of learning in our schools."—Bekker, 2012

There are several basic supervisory fundamentals that clearly demonstrate to teachers that the supervisor desires to support the teachers and their individual instructional growth.

Building an Effective Observation Culture

1. First and foremost, teachers should be thoroughly familiar with the purpose of the observation process. Every opportunity to discuss the process as a staff development tool should be taken. Whether it be in faculty meetings, small group discussions, or informal chats, time should be spent on creating an understanding of the process and a cultural belief that observations result in increased pedagogical effectiveness.

2. To ensure that observations focus on how to support the teacher, they should be conducted as early in the school year as possible so they can be helpful to the teacher. Initial observations should be implemented early in the year (e.g., new teachers should be observed by September 30), to give teachers and supervisors ample time to support and implement instructional recommendations.

3. Multiple observations should have ample space between them to allow for teacher implementation of recommendations. For example, new teachers need significant support in making their instructional decisions. Observing once a month, with multiple lesson plan workshops, peer support, and supervisory assistance between observations, will enable the supervisor to gauge the level of growth and identify future professional development needs.

4. To maximize sustained professional growth, observations should be conducted in varied lesson types (i.e., group lessons, pre- and post-test days, constructivist lessons, administration of a test, etc.). The rule of thumb is if it is worth class time, provide instructional support!

> *It is the work [principals] do that enables teachers to be effective—as it is not just the traits that teachers bring, but their ability to use what they know in a high-functioning organization that produces student success. And it is the leader who both recruits and retains high quality staff—indeed, the number one reason for teachers' decisions about whether to stay in a school is the quality of administrative support—and it is the leader who must develop this organization.—Darling-Hammond, et al. 2007*

Pre-Observation Supervisory Practices

1. Supervisors must do their homework, too! Reviewing previous end-of-year evaluations, as well as midyear reviews, will allow the supervisor to become familiar with each teacher's established goals. Prior observations are to be reviewed carefully, with particular attention paid to the recommendation areas. Was the teacher successful with implementation? Did the supervisor provide enough support for implementation?

2. Since new and weak teachers need additional support, the clinical supervision model can be extremely effective. Prior to the observation, a conference with the teacher to review how the lesson plan was created and how it aligns with the curriculum and state standards, as well as how it addresses students' instructional needs and preferences, creates a professional dialogue for professional decision making. This is an excellent opportunity for the supervisor to "teach."

My devotion to the clinical supervision process at the school was the single greatest illustration of my commitment to function as an instructional leader.—DuFour, 2002

How to Observe the Lesson

1. The observation serves as a springboard for the discussion of the principles and practices of sound and effective instruction. Never say, "When I come into your classroom, this is what I want to see!" It is not what the supervisor wants to see that results in the delivery of effective instruction. It is the utilization of research-based pedagogical practices coupled with a rigorous curriculum that creates high levels of student achievement (Schmoker, 2002). Keep in mind that this process is part of an overall supervisory plan that supports the professional growth of this teacher. The observation is a snapshot which provides the supervisor with an opportunity to reinforce effective practices while determining what kinds of additional ways a teacher can be professionally sustained.

2. Observations can be nerve-wracking for even the best teachers. The supervisor can minimize tension for the teacher by listening attentively, smiling, and saying a few encouraging words at the end of the lesson. Never take over the class. Avoid grimaces, frantic writing, or any intrusive action.

"Observations are best approached as a supportive and collaborative process. Your effectiveness as a teacher of teachers is greatly enhanced by building a high level of trust with your teachers and encouraging in them a spirit of self-analysis and reflection."—Coppola, Scricca, & Connors, 2004

---

3. To provide each teacher with valuable professional feedback, each observation must last for the complete lesson. Observing the teacher's lesson plan and its execution in its entirety is the only way to gather enough data to analyze a lesson's effectiveness.

4. Enter the classroom before the bell and sit in the back of the room. Supervisors must respect the rules we expect our students and teachers to respect.
5. Take copious notes with particular attention to lesson elements and the students' reaction to each teacher action. The better the notes, the greater the ability to successfully analyze the lesson.
6. Instruction is all about student engagement. Watch them!
7. Before leaving the classroom, view some student notebooks, student work, or project, whatever the class was engaged in, to ascertain the level of student understanding.

Supervisory Preparation for the Post-Observation Conference

1. The post-observation conference is the most important part of the observation process. It is here that the lesson can be cooperatively analyzed and discussed in a professional atmosphere.

   Create a professional learning culture in the school. . . . Teachers and principals need preparation and support to improve their skills at observing classrooms; giving frank and honest feedback; and assessing unit plans, tests, and data on student learning. The principal needs to be the "chief learner" in this regard. . . . The goal is to create a culture in which nondefensive analysis of student learning is "the way we do things around here."—Marshall, 2005

2. During this conference, the supervisor must clearly demonstrate to the teacher that instructional improvement is of the highest priority in the supervisor's pyramid of responsibility by conducting the post-observation with twenty-four hours. This timeline reinforces the importance of the process to the teacher.
3. Just as we expect teachers to plan for their lessons, so must supervisors plan for the post-observation conference. In preparing a post-observation conference, identify specific goals for teacher growth, areas of lesson strength, and areas that need improvement.
4. Additionally, the supervisor's lesson plan must include thought-provoking questions to foster the teacher's critical analysis of the lesson, resource materials, data from the lesson, and a plan for continuous support. The primary role of the supervisor during

the conference is to build the teacher's ability for constant self-evaluation and self-reflection.

Conducting the Post-Observation Conference

1. Analysis of the lesson is a cooperative undertaking. Have the teacher appraise all lesson elements, providing evidence from the lesson, teacher action-student response, to support findings on how effective each lesson element was.
2. Supervisors need to avoid attitudes of paternalism or condescension. As an instructional leader for the department/school, the supervisor is always a teacher!
3. Seek as many commendations and recommendations as possible from the teacher. Be a good listener, offering suggestions at times, but always facilitating the teacher's self-evaluation of the lesson. Why a practice is effective is as important to discuss as why a practice is ineffective. If we want teachers to repeat effective practices, they need to thoroughly understand why the practice is effective.
4. Effective teaching skills take time to develop, hone, and enhance. There are many aspects of instructional development because teaching is a complex skill. Therefore, areas for improvement need to be carefully chosen. The teacher needs to possess a foundation of good teaching.

   For example, if a teacher needs additional support in creating lesson objectives and lesson-starting activities, recommendations that focus on advanced questioning techniques might not be appropriate at that time. Recommendations should build on that foundation and be limited to two or three throughout the year.
5. Support recommendations with research, sound educational practices, and articles. It is not about what the supervisor wants to see; it is about effective educational practice.

Professional Development for Supervisors on Implementing the Observation Process

A professional culture where observations are viewed as helpful, are supportive, and result in improved instructional practice as the ultimate goal of strong supervision. To accomplish this, however, supervisors need the same kinds of support and professional development that teachers receive for instructional improvement.

> *Observation enables a supervisor to put a mirror of the classroom up to the teacher who can then attend to matters previously unknown. Several studies have shown that teachers often change instructional behaviors on their own after their classrooms have been described to them by an observer. The mirror can often be the stimulus for change. The observer must be careful in using interpretations, because such value judgments can actually cloud the mirror and prevent the teacher from seeing his or her own image. At all times, the observer needs to distinguish description from interpretation when recording and explaining events to the teachers.—Glickman, Gordon, & Ross-Gordon, 2009*

Professional development for supervisors on the observation process needs to be focused and continuous. Consider the following:

- *Observation of supervisors conducting post-observation conferences*—Just as we observe teachers in their classrooms to support instructional improvement, so must we observe supervisors administering the observation process to support supervisory improvement. An expert school leader can accompany a school supervisor, observing the actual lesson (Was the supervisor properly prepared for the observation? Did the supervisor record the appropriate classroom data?). Discuss the lesson with the supervisor after the actual observation, considering how the supervisor will plan for the post-observation conference. Observe the post-observation conference, then follow up with the supervisor with a post-observation conference between the expert school leader and supervisor (Did the supervisor effectively promote the teacher's ability to self-reflect on the lesson? Were the goals for the conference achieved by the supervisor?).
- *Workshops*—Providing supervisors with ongoing workshops on each aspect of the observation process will promote a culture that clearly says, "Supervisors are expected to hone their supervisory skills just as teachers are expected to hone their teaching skills." Building a common body of knowledge related to the observation

process, a common administration of the process, and a devotion to continually strengthen the skills needed to effectively support instruction should be the nucleus of these workshops.

- *Group observations*—In a very successful high school in New York, it is not unusual for the principal to ask for a teacher volunteer to be observed by the entire supervisory cabinet. The practice is a simple one. Members of the cabinet observe the teacher. They then analyze the lesson as a group. The teacher's supervisor conducts the post-observation conference, but it is recorded. This is then played for the entire cabinet and it analyzes the effectiveness of the post-observation conference. (What kind of planning does this supervisor do for the post-observation conference? What kind of planning does the teacher do for this conference? What does this planning say about their view of the process? What occurred during the conference that indicated there existed a cooperative spirit between supervisor and teacher? How did this supervisor foster the teacher's self-analysis of the lesson?).

This kind of supervisory professional development results in a culture in which instruction is supported and nurtured, where all professionals, teachers and supervisors alike, partake in a process that will result in improved instructional performance for the benefit of the students they serve. When teachers value the observation process because their instructional practices improve, its purpose is inherently understood and valued.

CONCLUDING THOUGHTS

- Observations should provide a rich professional development experience for teachers.
- The distinction between observation and evaluation must be clearly articulated and reflected in supervisory practice.
- Supervisors must convey to the teachers the pre-observation, observation, and post-observation practices that will be valued and employed.

- Supervisors must plan appropriately for post-observation conferences and immerse themselves in continuous professional development to improve their observation skills.

FOR REFLECTION

Based on ISLLC standard 2, as a school leader how do you create an
observation process that supports teachers' abilities to self-reflect on
their lessons while utilizing the process for continuous, individualized
professional development?

8

PROFESSIONAL DEVELOPMENT FOR THE LEADERSHIP TEAM

A Paradigm That Works!

It is possible to create systemic learning opportunities for school leaders that help them develop the complex skills needed to lead and transform contemporary schools.

—Darling-Hammond et al., 2007

Districts and schools must create a culture that respects, supports, and nurtures professional development as an essential mechanism toward continuous school improvement. This necessitates that these professional learners, serving at various levels in the school and district organization, from leadership to teachers to support staff, are immersed in a learning milieu.

In order for professional development to become embedded in school culture, it must result in improved employee performance. If professional development results in improved skills, improved job satisfaction will likely follow. The happier and more productive employees are, the greater and more effective their contributions to the organization will be.

DOES THIS SOUND FAMILIAR?

The new superintendent enters his assignment with great expectations. Unfortunately, he soon realizes that the very dedicated leadership group—principals, assistant principals, and even district leaders—has been severely neglected. Clearly, just as there was no effective leadership for the teachers and students, the leaders themselves had no common goals or focus and were lacking quality professional experiences.

It was evident that instructional supervision was not based on specific instructional goals. The supervisors did not have a strong working knowledge of how to observe teachers. They did not know how to guide teachers to reflect on their own teaching. Many of them had a strong base of knowledge of the curriculum, but they could not merge it with an effective supervisory paradigm that was aimed at improving instruction.

They did not know how to use the observation process to identify common instructional curriculum strengths and weaknesses or how to connect instructional strategies with curriculum content. The superintendent needed to develop a plan to create an instructional vision for the district's leaders and generate professional development that would produce highly trained observers.

Exploration into district leadership structures can reveal many actions or non-actions that contribute to teachers not recognizing that the instructional leadership team is a partner in their success. Common district leadership issues can include a lack of philosophical purpose, a constant turnover in administrative leadership, instructional supervision that has been punitive rather than supportive, and benign neglect toward the professional development of district leaders.

> *Successful districts give leaders and teachers the support and training they need to succeed.—DeVita, 2004*

DETERMINING THE PROFESSIONAL DEVELOPMENT NEEDS OF THE LEADERSHIP TEAM

Too often district leadership creates professional development mandates without gathering data on the needs of the leaders. To produce an effective professional development plan for leaders requires the gathering of specific data on supervisory behaviors and skills. These data can result in producing the types of professional development activities that will yield improved leadership performance.

To ascertain the level of district and school leadership expertise, engaging in the following activities can provide the data that will result in the determination of real leadership competence:

- Read all recent (up to three years) end-of-year evaluations that were conducted on district and school leaders. Create an individualized group list of strengths and weaknesses as cited by the evaluator. Please note that the quality of the evaluator must be taken into consideration when determining the efficacy of these reports.
- Read all recent (up to three years) end-of-year evaluations and teacher observations that each district and school leader wrote. Analyze each report to determine the quality of the reports: the level of instructional understanding, the use of a common body of district language, the application of effective supervisory processes, the use of a rubric for determining level of performance, and the application of a supervisory timeline that supports teacher implementation.
- Review the quality and quantity of past professional development activities for the leadership team by analyzing district initiatives, in-service course offerings, out-of-district workshops and conferences, and active memberships in professional organizations.
- Analyze student achievement data on local, state, and national levels. Are there curriculum and/or pedagogical issues that are evident in your analysis?

"The professional development efforts that appeared to provide the most meaningful support were those that were (1) focused on the instructional needs and goals of supervisors and principals, (2) sustained over time, (3) differentiated according to the skills and experience of personnel and the needs of the schools under their aegis, and (4) evaluated on how they affected student performance. These practices appeared more likely to help supervisors grow as instructional leaders and for students to benefit academically."—Corcoran et al., 2013

- Compare and contrast student achievement data findings with teacher data findings. Is there a correlation between teacher weaknesses and student achievement results? Do certain subject areas reveal more deficits than others?
- Meet with all district and school leaders both in groups and individually to determine how they made their supervisory decisions. Asking questions such as "What is your primary role?" "What kinds of skills do you need to effectively do your job?" and "How has the district supported your quest for improved performance?" provides anecdotal evidence to support your findings.
- Meet with teachers in groups as well as individually to determine the quality of instructional support received. Asking questions such as "Were expectations for teacher performance clearly articulated?" and "Is the observation process valued as a professional development activity?" can further your understanding of the quality of the instructional leadership team.

In essence, leaders must model what they expect their supervisors to demonstrate every day in their work with their teachers. Gathering data from various sources to inform supervisory decisions is as important as gathering data to inform the decisions teachers make in their classrooms.

Recently, Standards for Professional Learning (see Appendix, p. 99) have been nationally promulgated. These standards were developed by Learning Forward, with contributions from forty professional associations and educational organizations. These standards can serve as a guide for district leaders in creating the kinds of professional activities that will strengthen and hone the daily and long-range performance of leaders.

LEADERS THAT LEARN!

Reviewing research on school leadership reveals that leaders who are immersed in learning are clearly more effective as leaders. The school community views them as knowledgeable and productive. Faculty perceive them as able to support and sustain them as effective professionals.

Leaders committed to their own professional development spend extensive time on their own learning. They are engrossed in their own scholarship, for example, through reading and research. To illustrate the importance of this, one New York City high school had the standard principal's office on the first floor, but on the second floor was a small principal's study where he/she could go, uninterrupted, to immerse himself/herself in reading and reflection and preparation and planning. This is not to say that principals should learn by themselves, but, quite the contrary, that there are varied ways to learn and some learning can and should be done independently.

Themes that characterize high performing schools: heavy investments and highly targeted professional development for teachers and principals in the fundamentals of strong classroom instruction . . . and a normative climate in which adults take responsibility for their own, their colleagues', and their students' learning.—Elmore, 2004

IMPLEMENTING A LEADERSHIP PROFESSIONAL DEVELOPMENT MODEL

Building a cadre of skilled instructional leaders who can inform and inspire a district and a school's educational team needs to become a major focus. We know that high-quality leaders will significantly impact student learning. Therefore, designing and scheduling a series of professional development activities and interventions for district and school leaders will result in broadening and strengthening the kinds of instructional and leadership skills that educational supervisors need to become outstanding leaders.

Creating any professional development plan demands specific focus on the skill and competency levels of the leadership group. Targeting identified skill needs is essential to providing a quality professional development program, but so, too, is creating learning opportunities that take into consideration how these leaders learn. Professional development, therefore, must be a two-pronged approach: What do we want our leaders to learn and how are we going to teach it?

———————————————————— ⌘ ————————————————————

"As educators plan for staff development, it is essential that they create . . . learning opportunities that are grounded in best research and practice. Knowledge about how adults learn should provide the basis for planning and implementing any professional development opportunities. Attention to . . . learning styles as being significant elements that impact staff development effectiveness has been found to be crucial by several researchers."—Scricca, 2009

———————————————————— ⌘ ————————————————————

Instructional leaders need to recognize that their professional development program is a main concern. When district leadership makes this leadership development plan a priority in their hierarchy of responsibility, leaders will recognize, embrace, and commit to their own growth. When supervisors recognize the district has made this a priority for them—meeting their individual needs, centering on sound supervisory practices while focusing on district goals—a culture of professional development is vitalized, sustained, and, in some cases, born.

Many would consider this approach a professional learning community. As DuFour and Eaker (1998) so aptly state, a professional learning community is "an environment that fosters mutual cooperation, emotional support, and personal growth as educators work together to achieve what they cannot accomplish alone." While this is a very effective approach, leadership growth activities need to be focused on the individual leader's needs as well as the group and district needs.

Components for leadership professional development can include:

- **Pre-school year retreats**—In the midst of the daily administration of a school, the day's work can easily distract leaders from their own professional growth. A retreat can be a perfect structure for eliminating these distractions, and for focused, uninterrupted self-improvement.

  First and foremost, as a result of a pre-semester retreat, each leader will enter the school year motivated, focused, and equipped with new skills. With high expectations for their own performance as well as those under their supervision, each leader is given an opportunity to dedicate a significant amount of time, with their colleagues, toward personal and professional growth.

"A retreat is an opportunity to engender creativity—a time to remove your nose from the grindstone and look to the hills, a chance to think about what ought to be—and devise steps to get there."—McCaffery, 1992

Retreats afford an occasion for timely professional development, team-building activities, action planning, and opportunities to network with other leaders and mentors. Providing a platform to build internal leadership capacity and creating a network of support, as well as learning and developing specific instructional and leadership strategies, are just some activities that can bolster and support the leadership team.

A *cautionary note*: At the end of the retreat, it is important to determine how the district will support and nurture their leaders and the decisions made during the retreat. Clearly, a long-range, post-retreat strategy can be powerful in providing ongoing growth plans and support for the leadership team.

- **Monthly professional development seminars**—Too often, administrative meetings become places where middle-level management sit and listen to directives. To provide a learning environment at every level, monthly meetings can be an opportunity for professional development focused on district goals.

  Monthly seminars can serve several purposes: strengthening the leadership team while building the professional relationships between and among them. For example, if a district wants to focus on the use of student data to inform instructional decisions, the leadership team may possess varied expertise in data usage.

  Choosing a book such as Schmoker's *Results Now* (2006) to be read, discussed, and analyzed by the group can begin the journey to create master data leaders. This should be augmented by reading related articles, attending conferences and workshops, and sharing anecdotal evidence of the implementation of the strategies learned through these seminars.

This can be a rich and influential avenue for developing and supporting leadership growth. As Bottoms and Schmidt-Davis (2010) discovered in their case studies of high-performing, high-engagement learning environments, there was evidence that educators who read together, led together.

> *Today's principals and superintendents are learning leaders: they participate in regular, collaborative, professional learning experiences to improve teaching and learning. They recognize their own need to develop a broad knowledge base in curriculum, instruction, and assessment, and they seek ongoing professional development activities to achieve that goal.—Educational Research Service, 1999*

- **Leadership observations**—The use of teacher observations to improve instruction is a common supervisory practice. Though viewed differently, it is essentially an individualized professional development tool to improve instructional practices (see chapter 7). It is daily support for their craft, teaching and learning.

  So, too, must we support our leaders. Replicating an "observation process" for leaders can provide the kind of individual, specialized support they need to master the various leadership skills critical to effective administration and supervision. Chapter 9 is devoted to this form of supervisory support.

> *Many experts believe principals do not have adequate access to professional development related to their roles as school leaders. —Mizell, 2010*

- **Peer observations**—Teaming more experienced school leaders with new leaders can provide an in-house mentorship that will result in improved leadership performance. However, this practice should be extended throughout the leadership team.

  Each leader has different strengths and weaknesses. Creating a peer observation program that enables school leaders to spend time with each other in their schools—working with each other, observing tasks, and conversing about common issues—can be a most worthwhile professional development activity.

- **Sustained professional development**—Too often, district-level administrators assume that principals know how to administer, to lead, and to inspire. Whether it is the hiring process, dealing with difficult employees, or making decisions, administrative preparation programs do not totally prepare and support leaders for the real life in schools.

  For example, hiring the best teachers is key to providing the best instruction for students, but little is done to help instructional leaders develop a philosophical base and organizational approach from which to hire, as was delineated in chapter 4.

  To ensure leaders hire the best teachers, professional development in this area can include providing in-depth workshops for all involved leaders. Conducting mock interviews, instructing them on how to train interview committees, or creating teacher induction programs that are part of an ongoing series of workshops can guarantee that leaders hire the most effective teachers.

  [Developing leaders is] your job. It should be one of the most important things you do, and for the best leaders (meaning those leaders that understand the importance of people to their organization), it is a pleasure to assist and watch others grow and develop. So coach and mentor them, give them stretch assignments, and allow them to take risks and sometimes fail.—Asmus, 2014

CONCLUDING THOUGHTS

- Professional development for school leaders is crucial to student success and must be embedded in the district's culture.
- Leadership growth opportunities must be based on data regarding the leaders' skills, competencies, and needs.
- The professional development plan for leaders should reflect diversity in its format and delivery.

FOR REFLECTION

Based on ISLLC standard 2, as a school leader analyze the quantity and quality of the annual professional development you have been engaged in. Consider how this can be improved for the following year.

9

LEADERSHIP OBSERVATIONS

Supporting Continuous Growth

Strong schools need strong principals, and strong principals need strong support from the people they report to in the district's central offices.

—Miller, 2014

Tiger Woods, a world-class golfer, devotes hours and hours of practice to keeping his skills at a top-notch level. His practice sessions are intense, focused on specific goals, and, more often than not, are from seven to eight hours in length. All to play the game of golf!

His daily routine not only includes spending time on the range hitting specific golf shots; rather it is a more global approach. His day includes a workout routine, putting practice, work on his short game, strategies for mental toughness, and, sooner or later, applying these practice goals on the golf course itself.

Interestingly, though he is an expert in his field, he has a coach at his side, giving feedback, lending support, and helping him identify his goals and how to reach them. Most importantly, this coach fosters and strengthens his student's ability to self-correct on the golf course during competition, the ultimate accomplishment in self-reflection.

Remarkably, when most people are asked who they would prefer to have as their coach—Tiger Woods or his coach—they choose Tiger Woods. But in reality, it is the coach who brings out the talent and ability that is undeveloped in people.

It is the professional instructor, one who has walked the walk, has amassed a high level of expertise in the discipline, has the "teaching" and "observation" skills to identify strengths and weaknesses, and has nurtured his or her "student's" ability to self-correct, reflect, and refine skills, that can help a leadership professional continue on a path toward excellence.

Regardless of the achievement level of their school, principals were telling us that they wanted more time with instructional superintendents so they could observe their practice and be a thought partner.—Patricia Slaughter, assistant superintendent, Denver Public Schools. Quoted in Gill, 2013.

UTILIZING LEADERSHIP OBSERVATIONS TO PROMOTE GROWTH IN SCHOOL LEADERS

What Are Professional Leadership Observations?

As described in chapter 7, teacher observations, though the purpose might be different from school to school or state to state, are an accepted supervisory activity for the improvement of professional practice. Conversely, supervisory observations are not universally identified or utilized for leadership growth.

As we know, leadership activities are varied and can be extremely complex. Activities can include but are not limited to:

- creating a mission and vision for the school,
- analyzing student and teacher achievement data,
- reviewing and assessing curriculum,
- creating relationships with various community groups,
- implementing and overseeing new initiatives such as the common core standards,
- observing teachers,

- conducting discipline hearings of students and staff,
- developing goals and objectives for school improvement and continued growth,
- designing faculty professional development, and
- simply planning the day's activities.

Given this extensive and complex list of activities, how would a leader know

- why and how to do these activities and
- whether these responsibilities are being conducted in the most efficient and effective way?

"All educators should take part in continuous learning and be open to having their ideas and practices subjected to the scrutiny of their colleagues.—Elmore, 2004

Observation of leadership activities can produce the same kind of professional growth in a leader that instructional observations can promote in teachers. However, just like in teacher observation, where the level of instructional need must be identified to provide effective support, so, too, must a leader of leaders identify at what level of effectiveness a leader is functioning.

Let's Start at the Very Beginning . . .

The Interstate School Leaders Licensure Consortium's first standard requires that candidates understand and collaboratively develop, articulate, implement, and steward a shared vision of learning for a school. Yet how do school leaders achieve this? Where do they begin? How does it become their first order of business without the help and support from a seasoned leader who can provide the guidance and wisdom to help a new school leader address this most important standard?

Who Should Observe Leaders?

Can someone who has never been a doctor observe an operation and give feedback to the surgeon for improvement? Can just anyone evaluate a blueprint for a building and offer an architect pragmatic solutions for improving its quality? Similarly, can someone who has never been a principal, analyze, support, and strengthen the skills essential to school building leadership? Hardly likely, but it is frequently the case in the education arena.

> *Having all been principals . . . deputies have both the content and leadership expertise we need [to support our principals].—Susan Cordova, chief academic officer, Denver Public Schools. Quoted in Gill, 2013.*

Leadership development demands the kinds of support and professional development opportunities that we have recently recognized as essential to teacher instructional growth. To accomplish this, we need experienced, effective school leaders who have a demonstrated track record of success. They need to offer a wealth of support to school building and district leaders, to be mentors of substance and skilled coaches who can provide ongoing sustenance to both new and experienced educational leaders.

Conducting Leadership Observations: How to Begin the Journey

The life of a principal is multifaceted and exhausting. In addition to supervising faculty and support staff, principals respond to students and parents, the community, the district office, and emergencies while keeping the focus on student achievement.

Additionally, recent research identifies specific personal and professional characteristics that effective leaders must possess or work on developing (Stronge, et. al, 2008). In order to master these skills and develop traits indispensable to a school leader's success, it is paramount that they receive ongoing support, advice, and feedback from highly qualified mentors in all aspects of their job responsibilities. Preparing leaders to be leaders of change who place the interests and needs of students first, while focusing on the teaching and learning process, is the primary responsibility of the mentor.

To support a building leader's professional growth, it is paramount that a district provides a supervisor who can first serve as a coach, mentor, and sounding board to the principal. This person needs to have the skills that enable them to provide continuous, worthwhile feedback to the principal.

As a principal, I was used to being in control and making decisions for my own school. I have to learn the balance between coaching and listening and directing and telling. I am not here to do the job for them. It's not an easy skill to learn when you're so familiar with the role that you are now supervising.—Jermall Wright, principal supervisor. Quoted in Gill, 2013.

These leadership professional development activities should include:

- spending significant time in the school with the principal to observe, analyze, and gather evidence of the principal's performance;
- creating or revising a mission and vision for the school;
- analyzing the principal's daily planning process to ensure proactive planning rather than managerial reactive responses;
- assisting the school leader in developing a professional identity through memberships, readings, workshops, and conferences, thereby addressing their own needs and serving as a role model for their faculty;
- assessing the political climate to determine how to best put forth the school's agenda;
- reviewing school data together to create strategies for instructional improvement;
- utilizing these data to co-observe instruction with the principal by developing a plan for improvement that addresses individual teachers and schoolwide instructional needs;
- analyzing observation reports to ensure they clearly address instructional successes, weaknesses, and future needs;
- planning and assessing faculty meeting agendas and professional development opportunities to ensure continuous focus on the teaching and learning process;
- developing the self-reflection skills essential to continuous professional growth.

*Under the direction of the mentor, the learner is given immediate access
to valuable insights and past experiences. Within mentoring relationships,
individuals are learning by doing and are able to practice what they are
learning.—"How Does Mentoring Help Leaders," 2008*

It Can't Be Just about Mentoring!

Supporting leadership development must be embedded in the culture of the district. Providing strong mentorship is a solid step in creating effective leaders but certainly not the only strategy. Developing opportunities to strengthen the building leadership corps and identifying future leaders are critical to the success of a school district.

The supervisors of school leaders have a responsibility to evaluate and support them. Having a conference at the end of the year to review student achievement data, goal attainment, community partnerships, professional development activities, and school culture and morale, as well as teachers' instructional improvement, are essential components of this evaluation discussion. However, to inform an evaluation that considers all the tasks and responsibilities of a school leader, an evaluator should gather data from and offer support to school leaders in a variety of tasks throughout the year.

These leadership observations can take a variety of forms, such as observing a

- principal's cabinet meeting or a departmental meeting
- leader conducting a post-observation conference
- parent-teacher night
- leader during the workday, focusing on their scheduled plan and priorities
- principal conducting a student suspension hearing
- graduation ceremony
- sporting event
- instructional or grade-level team meeting
- schoolwide professional development activity
- curriculum meeting to common core and science, technology, engineering and mathematics (STEM) initiative
- observation reports

For example, after providing staff development in the classroom observation process to school leaders, a supervisor could be observed by another school leader or evaluator while conducting the post-observation conference. How the post-observation conference was conducted (How proficiently did the observer plan for this conference?) and the teacher's involvement in the lesson analysis (How did the supervisor stimulate the teacher's self-reflection skills?) can be the focus of a post-observation conference between the evaluator and school leader. This model, the same as a teacher observation model, creates an individualized opportunity to improve observation skills, thereby influencing teacher instructional improvement.

Culture of Learning

Providing a continuous professional development culture for leadership requires each building and district school leader to create a set of personal professional goals that they have identified as areas for growth and improvement. These articulated goals then serve as the nucleus around which all professional development activities within and outside the district will revolve. These activities must also be aligned with the district and school strategic plan.

A district culture that focuses on leadership professional development should include:

- *A leadership induction program*—Just as we provide for teachers an orientation, ongoing workshops, and an introduction to the policies and goals of a district, so, too, must we provide this level of support to our new district/school leaders.

"Induction is a multidimensional process that orients new principals to a school and school system while strengthening their skills and dispositions to be an educational leader.' —Villani, 2006

- *The establishment of personal leadership goals*—The efficacy of goal setting has been documented by countless academic studies in every field imaginable, demonstrating its importance in improving performance. Therefore, setting the foundation for a new leader requires self-examination of strengths and weaknesses. After creating goals, the leader must have the ability to attain them. As Peter Drucker (1993) has said, goals must be measurable and challenging but attainable.

"One must look inward to understand what it is they truly want to accomplish. Setting personal goals requires discipline, time, and a desire to make personal change."—Covey

---

- **Reading together, leading together**—Often, new leaders have common concerns and skill development needs. Identify books, articles, and journals for new leaders that provide research, guidance, and expertise in their recognized areas of interest and need. This focused reading group, chaired by members of the group, will generate an academic atmosphere in which new leaders can discuss topics in a supportive, collegial environment while learning skills essential to their success.
- **Professional life outside of the district**—On the national, state, and local stages, there is an abundance of professional organizations that provide varying levels of support for school leaders. So how does a new leader choose which and how many to join?

  Many leaders remain with their past professional organizations as well as join organizations related to their specific job (e.g., National Association of Secondary School Principals for middle/high school principals). The key in membership is to be an active member. This could involve the regular reading of journals, attending workshop and seminar offerings at every level—local, state, national, and international—becoming involved in the governance of the professional organization, and participating in Job-Alike networks.
- **Developing a leadership "farm" system**—Induction programs, district leadership workshops, orientations, literature circles, and any other leadership activity can include prospective leadership candidates. Within every district exists new, upcoming talent. What

better way is there to prepare for future leadership positions! Involve them in district leadership development events and activities. It gives the candidates an opportunity to determine if this is truly the path they will choose while offering the district an opportunity to provide further development activities for the leaders of the future.

Leadership training should not end when principals are hired. It should continue with high-quality mentoring for new principals and with professional development for all principals to promote career-long growth in line with the evolving needs of schools and districts.—Wallace Foundation, June 2008

Districts that incorporate leadership professional growth activities will gain a cadre of leaders that are highly skilled. Additionally, these school leaders will serve as role models for the larger school community.

CONCLUDING THOUGHTS

- Observation of leadership activities is essential for leaders' professional growth.
- Leaders need ongoing support, advice, and feedback from highly qualified mentors.
- Support for leadership development must be imbedded in the culture of the district.

FOR REFLECTION

Based on ISSLC standard 5, which encourages leaders to model principles of self-awareness and reflective practice, how do the leadership observations outlined in this chapter support this standard?

10

STRONG LEADERS SUSTAIN STRONG SCHOOLS

The leaders who work most effectively, it seems to me, never say "I." And that's not because they have trained themselves not to say "I." They don't think "I." They think "we"; they think "team." They understand their job to be to make the team function. They accept responsibility and don't sidestep it, but "we" gets the credit. . . . This is what creates trust, what enables you to get the task done.

—Peter Drucker, 1993

As we bring this book to a close, the question of "where do you go from here?" arises. How do you process, digest, reflect on, and then implement all that we have written in the preceding pages? Probably the best advice we can give is simply to start with you. Take stock of who you are as an educator—what you believe, what you value, what your commitment is to your students, your passion as a lifelong learner, and your personal qualities. The person you are will drive the educational leader you can be.

Research has evidenced the important characteristics of effective leaders. These leadership characteristics are outlined in the following pages. As you move from "I" to "we" in your effort to build a strong leadership team and a strong district and school, developing those characteristics essential to leadership will be your ultimate challenge.

STRONG LEADERS ASK FOCUSED QUESTIONS

The most successful leaders utilize questions to involve their staff, encourage teamwork, and create solutions to problems together. Building relationships like these requires engaging staff in different ways, empowering them to be part of the processes that make schools effective. These leaders know that questions are an effective way to connect with people. When we ask a question of a teacher, we send a strong signal that what he or she thinks matters. Good questions generate thought, focus, and action from the listener. They also convey respect, which leads to trust.

> *Exceptional leaders today swallow their egos and ask. That's because exceptional leaders realize that leadership comes from developing other egos, not their own.*—Cohen, 2010

Math Director Rosa prepared well for each post-observation conference. Not only did she carefully analyze the data she collected during the lesson, but she spent time reflecting on her own role as the math supervisor. She asked herself "How can I get this teacher to reflect on the decisions she made in teaching this lesson?" and "What can I do to bring this teacher to a higher level of effectiveness?" As a result, she prepared a series of questions to be asked during the post-observation conference, to engage this teacher in the process of self-reflection. These questions included "Why did you choose this objective for this lesson?" "How did you know that your students achieved this objective?" "What evidence during the lesson supports that your students achieved this goal?" and "What might you change to make this lesson more effective?"

After reflecting on these questions privately, Director Rosa incorporated them into her post-observation meeting with the teacher to gain a more focused perspective and enrich the professional exchange of ideas. The members of her department often commented that such questions empowered them, encouraged them to examine their own practices, and enabled them to solve instructional problems.

STRONG LEADERS HOLD HIGH EXPECTATIONS FOR THEMSELVES AND OTHERS

The strongest leaders are cognizant of the larger community that exists beyond the school walls. Everyone watches their leaders—their reactions to events, their tone of voice with a student, how they listen to a parent complaint, their demeanor during a school crisis. Great leaders know that they must exemplify the behavior that is expected of all. They know they are role models.

As the new leader of an underachieving elementary school, Principal Clare spent her first three months observing classes, attending parent-teacher meetings, participating in child study team consultations, and visiting the faculty room for informal discussions regarding school achievement and culture. Her focus was to gather data so she could share her findings with all stakeholders, particularly the faculty, and with them, design a strategic plan for improvement.

During her observations, it was quite apparent that a lack of respect was a significant part of the school's culture. Teachers did not respect the parents, each other, and worst of all, the students themselves. Yelling was commonplace at meetings. Teachers frequently exhibited unprofessional behavior in the classroom, particularly in how they spoke to students. Additionally, it was not uncommon that faculty did not bother to attend important meetings designed to help students' academic success. Parents complained that teachers generally did not return their phone calls or address their concerns.

Utilizing the data she gathered, she designed a sensitivity training. She then conducted workshops for both faculty and parents. During these workshops, she modeled situations and acceptable behaviors. Her efforts did not stop here. She realized that her every thought, word, and deed would be scrutinized by parents, faculty, and students.

She recognized this as an important part of the initiative to improve the school's culture—she must be a role model of professionalism. Her very presence throughout the day and in a variety of situations, whether it be dealing with an irate parent or a student who needed to be disciplined, demonstrated that these situations could be dealt with professionally and with dignity and respect for all. Being the role model helped change and remold this school's culture.

Principals, by virtue of their roles as instructional leaders and moral agents in their schools, serve as models for respect, understanding, sensitivity, and appreciation of others. This point isn't negotiable. Principals are role models.—Stronge, Richard, & Catano, 2008

STRONG LEADERS ENCOURAGE OTHERS TO EXPERIMENT, TAKE RISKS, AND ACCEPT FAILURE

Improving schools requires seeking innovative and creative ideas to change the status quo. This kind of improvement requires taking risks. As we all know, risk-taking involves mistakes and sometimes even results in failure. However, great leaders examine these creative solutions, learn from them, encourage inventive and inspired thinking, and, ultimately, support rather than criticize taking a risk.

The administrative team felt like they had won the lottery when it was announced that Superintendent James was to lead their team! They had heard of him by reputation. He was a passionate, inspiring leader who valued his "team" and supported creative thinking. Although many griped about how hard they worked to meet his standards, none ever said a negative word about his leadership.

From the very first cabinet meeting, members of the team knew their lives as school leaders were on an upward climb to personal growth and excellence. This superintendent never wasted meeting time on "housekeeping" tasks—all of that could be done by email or memo—rather, every interaction was directed to improving the climate of the school and the development of the teachers, and, ultimately, to creating programs and solutions to bolster student achievement.

He personally spent time with each leader to help develop their goals, monitor their progress, challenge their thinking, and collaborate on resolving their problems. He encouraged out-of-the-box thinking, creative solutions to issues, and implementing new ideas.

The schools' leaders knew if their new ideas failed, the superintendent's response would be one of support. He would work with them to figure out why a new idea had failed and decide what they could learn from the failed innovation. Perhaps most importantly, he courageously defended their work and their decisions to others, provided it was all in the best interest of the students.

In organizations that are committed to building a risk-taking culture, one thing must remain consistent, and that is the leader's response to risk. Constant, predictable reactions and support—despite the outcomes—is the only way to ensure the significant individual and organizational shifts required to institutionalize innovation and achieve long-term, sustainable growth.—Giulioni, 2013

STRONG LEADERS AREN'T AFRAID TO ADMIT MISTAKES

Do the best leaders make mistakes? You bet they do! Trying new ventures, taking risks, or just making a wrong decision, since we are all human, will result in mistakes. But how we deal with our mistakes will determine how every constituency will view our leadership. Accepting responsibility for our mistakes, acknowledging them, and using them as opportunities for future learning frames our leadership. Being forthright about our decisions, both good and bad, engenders respect and trust and serves as a positive model for others.

The school was preparing for state registration. The special education department had never passed a review. The principal had given all the support the assistant principal needed to get this department prepared for this state examination.

There was a great deal of mutual respect between the special education teachers and the assistant principal. The faculty worked tirelessly for six months in preparation for the visit. Unfortunately, three weeks before the visit, the assistant principal took ill and had to be hospitalized. She worked from her hospital bed. She had asked her teachers to submit the last classroom-administered test for her review. From the hospital, where she reviewed them, she wrote an evaluation on each test, then emailed each teacher their evaluation.

The following week she returned to work to discover that the teachers were angry that she had sent the evaluations without a personal, professional discussion with each teacher. One teacher said to her that they felt betrayed after all the work they had done that they found this evaluation in their inbox.

After thoughtful consideration, she realized she had made a serious mistake. She had a golden rule that she never put anything in writing unless she had a discussion with the teacher. In the interest of expediency rather than professionalism, she had sent the evaluations.

She called an emergency meeting and asked the teachers to bring the evaluations. At the meeting, she asked them to pass them to her. She apologized for thinking of the state registration process rather than them and proceeded to rip up the evaluations. "I made a mistake."

"Leaders should embrace mistakes, not only for themselves, but for their team as well. If you as the leader will admit you're wrong, and then walk your team through a process of what you learned and what you would do differently, you will have raised your entire team to a new level. Not only an experience for you, but with the example you are setting, you will lead your team to new heights."—Thomas, 2011

STRONG LEADERS DEMONSTRATE CARE AND UNDERSTANDING

Too often leaders forget that faculty and staff have a personal life outside of school. As we well know, everyday life comes with problems and stressors that can affect how we do our work in schools. It is important that leaders recognize, understand, and support their staff through life's challenges.

Balancing one's personal life with the demands of a professional career can be made easier when the school leader appreciates how delicate a balance this is. Compassion and empathy play a significant role in providing the kind of leadership that generates a dedicated staff.

Carrie returned from maternity leave in the middle of the year. She left a baby and her two-year-old in the care of her husband, who worked evenings.

An excellent high school foreign language teacher, she returned to her assignment a bit exhausted but nonetheless committed to her students. Her classes had two different teachers before she returned to her assignment. Needless to say, her classes were a bit disorganized and had not covered the curriculum they were supposed to in the previous six months.

Carrie worked tirelessly to bring her students back on track. She planned creative, rigorous lessons, staying up all hours of the night to vary her instructional approaches for her students.

One morning, about three months after she returned to work, she was entering the school, saw the principal, and started to cry. The principal brought her into her office and had another teacher cover her class. Carrie was exhausted! With two small children at home, a husband that worked at night, and the comprehensive planning she needed to create for her classes, she had no time for herself. She was so overwhelmed she told the principal, "I don't even have time to get my hair cut!"

After Carrie composed herself, the principal talked with her about some strategies that she suggested a working mother could employ. When Carrie was ready, she returned to her classes the next period.

Meanwhile, the principal called Carrie's husband, expressed her concern for Carrie's well-being, and asked her husband if he would be able to get a babysitter for the afternoon. After he arranged for the afternoon childcare, the principal called a friend who was a hair stylist and made an appointment for Carrie.

To this day, Carrie continues to tell the story of the most compassionate principal she ever worked for!

Servant leadership . . . is strongly based in ethical and caring behaviour and enhances the growth of workers while improving the caring and quality of organizational life. . . . Characteristics of the servant leader . . . include: listening, empathy, healing, awareness, . . . foresight, . . . commitment to the growth of people, and building community.—Spears, 2010

STRONG LEADERS UNDERSTAND HOW TECHNOLOGY IMPACTS HOW WE LIVE AND WORK

This isn't the same as technical expertise. We are not saying that it's important for educational leaders to all of a sudden become "techies." However, school leaders do need to understand the overall technology landscape and how it is impacting the way we learn, work, and live.

Effective school leaders are committed to learning and utilizing technology, whether they are digital natives or digital immigrants themselves

(Prensky, 2001). They understand that it is not so much the technology itself that is important but rather how we utilize this expertise to create a technologically savvy school culture.

They know the effective use of technology will enable faculty and students to access information. Effective school leaders understand that technology will enable staff and students to communicate in a most efficient manner and develop the kinds of skills essential to a global society, while promoting faculty implementation of technology through professional development.

Addressing the needs of all students through technology use is a long-term and system-wide effort. School leaders, therefore, are expected to possess not only general leadership skills but also technology leadership skills.
—Valdez, 2004

Plainfield High School abounds with technology. Each classroom is fully equipped with SmartBoards, Internet access, three laptops, and a printer. Yet not one classroom is using this technology. Instruction is basically chalk and talk.

Louis Middle School abounds with technology as well. In addition to the technology that Plainfield has, each student has a laptop that has their textbooks installed. There is also a website for each class and a school management system that parents can easily access to follow what their children are doing in class and the class requirements. Classrooms are abuzz with students creating multimedia presentations, responding to problem-solving activities by researching on their computers, and communicating with students from all over the world on similar projects. These classrooms are similar to what we see in offices all across America.

Why does this happen? Why is there such a stark difference between these two schools? Let's visit the principals' offices of Plainfield and Louis.

The Plainfield principal's office is completely devoid of any technology activity. Yes, there is a desktop computer in his office, but it is rarely used. His secretary prints out his calendar in the morning as well as his emails. He communicates with his staff through a newsletter that is placed in the teachers' mailboxes. There is no school website since he believes that parents should come to the school to access information or read the school mailings.

In contrast, the Louis principal's office is quite a different place. In addition to a laptop computer, this principal has a personal tablet to access student and faculty schedules, keep in contact with his office as he is visiting classrooms, and send emails to parents with their child's latest work, downloaded when he visited a classroom. He lives and breathes technology. He is a role model for technology making life easier and learning accessible.

"Leaders passionately believe they can make a difference. They envision the future, creating an ideal and unique image of what the organization can become. Through their magnetism and quiet persuasion, leaders enlist others in their dreams. They breathe life into their visions and get people to see exciting possibilities for the future."—Kouzas & Posner, 2014

STRONG LEADERS DON'T ASSUME THEY KNOW EVERYTHING

The best leaders continue to grow themselves professionally. Through their continued quest for knowledge, they become role models for the people they lead. Similarly, their supervisors understand that the emphasis in professional development should be to support an experienced leader faced with the day-to-day realities of leadership practice. Consider this scenario:

The essence of being a leader is the willingness to continue to be a learner. If you are not willing to continue learning, then you have no business being a leader, especially in education.—Richardson, 2014

Assistant Superintendent Diana held very high expectations for her middle-management team in terms of continuing their professional growth. She supported their requests to attend conferences and workshops directly related to their personal work goals. She used meeting time to delve into all aspects of teaching and learning. She initiated book talks and peer observations to consider and observe best practices. She arranged for visitations to other schools and programs for them to collect data on instructional practices that would then be critically examined within their cabinet meetings.

*Imagine her reaction one morning to find a sign posted on her chair by the superintendent stating "ABDs (**All But Dissertation**) are worthless"! Here was a not-so-subtle message that while she had been touting, supporting, and even demanding the continuous professional growth of those she supervised, she was in fact neglecting the completion of her own doctoral dissertation! Her credibility as an outstanding leader would be at stake if she allowed the clock to run out on this professional accomplishment. Needless to say, Doctor Diana got the message!*

"Great leaders continue to improve themselves in every possible way. The person who thinks he is an expert has a lot more to learn. Never stop learning. Be receptive to everyone's perceptions and information from around the world and beyond. Grow, grow, grow. . . . Learn, learn, learn."—Banks, 2014

CONCLUDING THOUGHTS

There are essential characteristics related to the success of strong school leaders:

- They cultivate interpersonal relationships by showing care and understanding, acting ethically with honesty and integrity, and recognizing their staff's accomplishments.
- They model specific behaviors by being flexible, adaptable, fair, and courageous.
- They keep the focus on what matters: the teaching and learning process.

FOR REFLECTION

Based on all ISSLC standards, a strong instructional leader should be guided by three personally reflective questions:

- What do I need to stop doing that is hindering instruction?
- What should I start doing to support teachers?
- What should I continue doing to help teaching and learning flourish in the classroom?

11

GOING THE DISTANCE

Becoming a Leader of Leaders

Reflection and inquiry are not practiced much: People everywhere are impeded from working together effectively by the conflicting views of the world. But the discovery of oneself, the ability to see something in your own behavior that was invisible to you before, and appreciation of what's productive and what's painful in your attitudes—awareness of these capabilities seems pretty intrinsic to the human condition

—Senge et al., 2006

There is no one way to lead. Every educational administrative graduate course of substance will expose you to a variety of leadership styles, from transactional leadership to transformational leadership. So then, which one should you adopt as your leadership approach?

This book offers a much different mindset. It is not about leadership styles—it's about effective leadership actions. There is no one way to become an effective educational leader. As leaders, we need to be aware of all the research on various leadership theories, however, just like teachers who are expected to diversify their teaching methods to students' learning styles, so must leaders adapt their styles to the needs of those we evaluate, and those we serve. It is much more complicated than applying a leadership theory to become a certain kind of leader.

Effective leaders understand this and, as a result, become leaders of leaders. Too often people are thrust into positions with little or no support and guidance. For example, a new principal is expected to know how to be a principal and is usually not provided with the ongoing professional development essential to becoming an adaptive leader. Effective leaders must possess many leadership qualities and skills. They must know how to apply those skills to different situations and teach and model them on a daily basis. This is an imperative! The road to improve student achievement is through the actions of quality leaders who create and support effective teachers.

In conclusion, it is essential to focus on the following:

- Teacher quality and effectiveness is the key to improved student learning. However, teachers need ongoing support from quality supervisors to learn what good teaching is, implement effective instruction, and receive quality professional development experiences.
- Teacher professional development is on the top of the list in every district across the country, but that is not true for leadership professional development. Conversely, the most effective districts and schools understand that leadership is key. They provide extensive, focused professional development for their district and school leaders.
- Everyone in a district must support principals. From the boardroom to the district office, the understanding of the research that principals are second only to effective teachers in improving student achievement must be the focus of all those making budget decisions and district policies. It is neither the Board of Education nor the superintendent who can change a school's culture and, ultimately, student achievement results. It is the principal!
- Quality school leaders must be hired through a focused, non-political process. Hiring committees must be trained, given a specific set of leadership criteria that match the school's needs, and understand that they do not hire but recommend. The best leaders are those who possess the qualities and skills that match the position's needs.
- Nepotism and cronyism can be the most destructive factor in a district's hiring practices. However, it can be eliminated through

a carefully constructed process that pre-identifies goals, leaders' characteristics, and skill sets that match the positions' needs.

- Research is very clear regarding instructional leadership. School leaders must make this their primary responsibility and most think they do. But to actively reflect on one's daily work and categorize it as an instructional or a management task will usually result in something much different than expected. Understanding what instructional leadership is and then placing it into practice is a task that must be examined daily by educational leaders if we intend to improve student achievement results.

- How often do we hear educators use the words observation and evaluation as synonyms? This clearly indicates a lack of understanding as to the purpose of classroom observations. Classroom observations are the foundation of teacher professional development and can provide a roadmap for continuous and focused pedagogical growth activities to further strengthen faculty skills.

- Building a culture of classroom observation as a professional development process requires ongoing leadership training. Too often the perception of the purpose of the classroom observation varies from leader to leader even within a district. Creating and imbedding a classroom observation philosophy and concomitant guidelines will ensure that classroom observations will result in improving faculty instructional growth.

- Creating a professional development paradigm for the leadership team can be an arduous task, but to move a district and school forward and improve student achievement, it is critical. This entails a careful review of leadership data, from student achievement results to reviews of leaders' annual evaluations and even teacher evaluations. This is a complex charge and no one instrument or data analysis will fully indicate your leaders' professional development needs. Your assessment demands a comprehensive, analytical approach to inform an inclusive, focused professional development program sustaining leadership growth.

- Just as we observe teachers in their classrooms, educational leaders need to be observed in their districts, in their schools, or in their departments. There are myriad leadership responsibilities that can be analyzed to determine what is effective and what can be improved. As leaders of leaders, we must observe them in various venues, provide constant feedback, and help them develop the kinds of self-reflection skills expected of all educators.

BECOME THE LEADER YOU WANT YOUR LEADERS TO BE!

APPENDIX

STANDARDS FOR PROFESSIONAL LEARNING

Learning Communities: Professional learning that increases educator effectiveness and results for all students occurs within learning communities committed to continuous improvement, collective responsibility, and goal alignment.

Leadership: Professional learning that increases educator effectiveness and results for all students requires skillful leaders who develop capacity and advocacy, and who create support systems for professional learning.

Resources: Professional learning that increases educator effectiveness and results for all students requires prioritizing, monitoring, and coordinating resources for educator learning.

Data: Professional learning that increases educator effectiveness and results for all students uses a variety of sources and types of student, educator, and system data to plan, assess, and evaluate professional learning.

Learning Designs: Professional learning that increases educator effectiveness and results for all students integrates theories, research, and models of human learning to achieve its intended outcomes.

Implementation: Professional learning that increases educator effectiveness and results for all students applies research on change and sustains support for implementation of professional learning for long-term change.

Outcomes: Professional learning that increases educator effectiveness and results for all students aligns its outcomes with educator performance and student curriculum standards.

REFERENCES

Asmus, Mary Jo. (2014, January 2). Developing leaders: It's your job [Blog post]. Retrieved from http://smartblogs.com/leadership/2014/01/02/develop ing-leaders-its-your-job/.

Banks, R. (2014). *The top 10 ways to improve your leadership skills.* International Cyber Business Services, Inc. Retrieved from http://www.icbs/kb/inspiration/kb-inspiraton-the-top-10-ways-to-improve-your-leadership.htm.

Bekker, T. (2012, September 19). *Seven steps to effective feedback.* Retrieved from http://connectedprincipals.com/archives/6335.

Berkowicz, J., & Myers, A. (2014, February 26). *Feedback as professional development.* Leadership 360, *Education Week.*

Bottoms, G., & Schmidt-Davis, J. (2010). *The three essentials: Improving schools requires district vision, district and state support and principal leadership.* Southern Regional Education Report (SREB).

Broad Foundation. (2006, September). *Improved principal hiring.* Retrieved March 10, 2014, from http://www.broadeducation.org/asset/1128-tntp improvedprincipalhiring.pdf.

Center for American Progress. *Increasing Principal Effectiveness.* (2011, March 24). Retrieved November 6, 2014 from https://www.americanprogress.org/issues/education/report/2011/03/24/9192/increasing-principal-effectiveness.

Chapman, J. D. (2005). *Recruitment, retention and development of school principals.* Educational Policy Series, International Institute for Educational Planning.

Chenoweth, K., & Theokas, C. (2011). *Getting it done: Leading academic success in unexpected schools.* Boston, MA: Harvard Education Press.

Clifford, M. (2012). *Hiring quality school leaders: Challenges and emerging practices.* Naperville, IL: American Institutes for Research. Retrieved February 22, 2012, from http://www.air.org/files/Hiring_Quality_School_Leaders.pdf.

Cohen, G. (2010, July/August). *Just ask leadership: Why great managers always ask the right questions.* Ivey Business Journal. Retrieved from http://iveybusinessjournal.com/topics/leadership/just-ask-leadership-why-great-managers-always-ask-the-right-questions#.VFCcKhYXK9o.

Collins, J. C. (2001). *Good to great: Why some companies make the leap and others don't.* New York, NY: Harper Business.

Coppola, A., Scricca, D. B., & Connors, G. E. (2004). *Supportive supervision: Becoming a teacher of teachers.* Thousand Oaks, CA: Corwin Press.

Corcoran, A., Casserly, M., Price-Baugh, R., Walston, D., Hall, R., & Simon, C. (2013, October). *Rethinking leadership: The changing role of principal supervisors.* The Wallace Foundation.

Council of State School Officers. (1996). *Interstate school leaders licensure consortium standards for school leaders.* Washington, DC: Author. Retrieved from www.ccsso.org/pdfs/isllcstd.pdf.

Covey, S. *The community online: How to set personal goals.* Retrieved November 6, 2014, from www.stephencovey.com/personal-goals/php.

Darling-Hammond, L., LaPointe, M., Meyerson, D., Orr, M. T., & Cohen, C. (2007). *Preparing school leaders for a changing world: Lessons from exemplary leadership development programs.* Stanford, CA: Stanford University, Stanford Educational Leadership Institute.

DeVita, M. C. (2004). Taking stock in education leadership: How does it really matter? In K. Leithwood, K. S. Louis, S. Anderson, & L. Wahlstrom, *How leadership influences student learning* (p. 3). Toronto, Canada: Ontario Institute for Studies in Education, Center for Applied Research and Educational Improvement.

DeVita, M. C. (2007). Getting principal preparation right. In L. Darling-Hammond et al. (2007). *Preparing school leaders for a changing world: Lessons from exemplary leadership development programs* (p. 3). Stanford, CA: Stanford University, Stanford Educational Leadership Institute.

Drucker, P. (1993). *Management: Tasks, responsibilities, practices.* New York, NY: Harper Business.

DuFour, R. (2002). *The learning-centered principal.* Educational Leadership, ASCD. Volume 59, no. 8, pp. 12–15.

DuFour, R., & Eaker, R. (1998). *Professional learning communities at work: Best practices for enhancing student achievement.* Bloomington, IN: National Educational Service.

Education Partnerships, Inc. (2013). *Importance of high expectations.* Retrieved from http://gearup.ous.edu/sites/default/files/Research-Briefs/ResearchBriefHighExpectations.pdf.

Educational Research Service. (1999). *Professional development for school principals.* The Informed Educator Series. Arlington, VA: Author.

Elmore, R. (2004). Building a new structure for school leadership. *School reform from the inside out: Policy, practice and performance.* Boston, MA: Harvard Education Press.

Ericsson, K. A., Prietula, M. J., & Cokely, E. T. (2007, July/August). The making of an expert. *Harvard Business Review.*

Freeley, M. E., & Scricca, D. (2012, April). Master leaders produce master teachers. *Principal Leadership* 40–45.

Gill, J. (2013, December). *Make room for the principal supervisors.* New York, NY: The Wallace Foundation.

Giulioni, J. W. (2013, August 8). Risky business: Strategies to encourage employee risk-taking [Blog post]. Retrieved May 27, 2014, from http://smartblogs.com/leadership/2013/08/08/risky-business-strategies-to-encourage-employee-risk-taking/.

Glickman, C., Gordon, S. P., & Ross-Gordon, J. (2009). *The basic guide to supervision and instructional leadership.* Boston, MA: Pearson.

Hallinger, P., & Heck, R. H. (1996). Reassessing the principal's role in school effectiveness: A review of empirical research, 1980–1995. *Educational Administration Quarterly, 32*(1), 5–44.

Hitt, D. H., Tucker, P., & Young, M. (2012). *The professional pipeline for educational leadership.* Charlottesville, VA: The University Council for Educational Administration.

Hollenbeck, G. P. (1994). *CEO selection: A street-smart review.* Greensboro, NC: Center for Creative Leadership.

Honig, M., Lorton, J., & Copland, M. (2009). *Urban district central office transformation for teaching and learning improvement: Beyond a zero-sum game,* Yearbook of the National Society for the Study of Education. Volume 108, no. 1, pp. 21–40.

How does mentoring help leaders and managers grow and develop? (2008). Retrieved on January 18, 2014, from http://www.insala.com/Articles/leadership-coaching/how-does-mentoring-help-leaders-and-managers-grow-and-develop.asp.

Hoy, W., & Tarter, J. (1995). *Administrators solving the problems of practice.* Boston, MA: Allyn and Bacon.

Knight, J. (2011). *Unmistakable impact: A partnership approach to dramatically improving instruction.* Thousnad Oaks, CA: Corwin Press.

Kouzes, J., & Posner, B. (2011, April 17). The best leaders are the best learners [Blog post]. Retrieved on February 19, 2014, from http://www.leadership challenge.typepad.com.

Kouzes, J., & Posner, B. (2011). *Head, heart and soul: Lessons from the leadership challenge forum, August 22, 2011.* Retrieved on February 19, 2014, from http://www.leadershipchallenge.typepad.com.

Kouzes, J., & Posner, B. (2014). *The five practices of exemplary leadership model.* Retrieved May 27, 2014, from http://www.leadershipchallenge.com/about-section-our-approach.aspx.

Leithwood, K., & Jantzi, D. (2000). The effects of transformational leadership on organizational conditions and student engagement with schools. *Journal of Educational Administration, 38*(2), 112–129.

Leithwood, K., Louis, K. S., Anderson, S., & Wahlstrom, K. (2004). *How leadership influences student learning.* New York: The Wallace Foundation. Retrieved April 8, 2014, from http://www.wallacefoundation.org/knowledge-center/school-leadership/key-research/Documents/How-leadership-influences-student-learning.pdf.

Lenz, B. (2010, April 25). How charter schools handle hiring teachers [Blog post]. Retrieved from http://www.edutopia.org/charter-schools-hiring-process-lenz.

Marshall, K. (2005, June). It's time to rethink teacher supervision and evaluation. *Phi Delta Kappan, 86*(10), 727–735.

Marzano, R., Pickering, D., & Pollack, J. E. (2001). *Classroom instruction that works: Research-based strategies for increased student achievement.* Alexandria, VA: ASCD.

McCaffery, J. (1992, January 1). *Planning and Implementing Retreats.* Retrieved July 25, 2014, from http://www.trg-inc.com/resources/articles/implementing-retreats.html.

Miller, W. President of The Wallace Foundation (2014, February 19). Wallace launches $24-million initiative for districts to strengthen supervisors of school principals in effort to improve student learning [web post by Mike Keaney]. Retrieved March 30, 2014, from http://www.schoolleadership20.com/forum/topics/wallace-launches-24-million-initiative-for-districts-to-strengthe

Mizell, H. (2010). *Why Professional Development Matters.* Ohio: Learning Forward. Retrieved July 14, 2014 from www.learningforward.org/advancing/whypdmatters.cfm.

No Child Left Behind (NCLB) Act of 2001, Pub. L. No. 107–110, § 115, Stat. 1425. 1425 (2002).

Page, B. (2002). *We get what we get*. Retrieved March 15, 2014, from http://www/teachers.net/gazette/DEC02/page.html.

Prensky, M. (2001). *Digital natives, digital immigrants*. MCV University Press. Volume 9, no. 5, 1–6.

Pursley, N. P. (2002, October). *Reflections on leadership*. USC Institute for Public Service and Policy Research—Public Policy in Practice.

Reeves, D. (2002). *The daily disciplines of leadership: How to improve student achievement, staff motivation and personal organization*. San Francisco, CA: Jossey-Bass.

Richardson, J. (2014, April). Learning to lead. *Phi Delta Kappan, 95*(7), 4.

Robinson, V., Lloyd, C., & Rowe, K. (2008). The impact of leadership on school outcomes: An analysis of the differential effects of leadership types. *Educational Administration Quarterly, 45*(5), 635–674.

Romano, V. (2012). *Secondary teachers' and their supervisors' perceptions of current and desired observation practices that promote instructional improvement*. Unpublished doctoral dissertation. Jamaica, NY: St. John's University.

Schmoker, M. (2002, May 1). *The Real Causes of Higher Achievement*. Retrieved August 8, 2014, from http://www.sedl.org/pubs/sedletter/v14n02/

Scricca, D. B. (2009). Give them what they want! Administrative guidelines for staff development based on secondary teachers' learning styles. *Long Island Education Review, 8*(2), 20–23.

Senge, P., et. al (2006). As cited in W. G. Cunningham & P. A. Cordeiro. *Educational leadership: A problem-based approach*. Boston, MA: Pearson.

Souba, W. (2006, January). Leadership values in academic medicine. *Academic Medicine, 81*(1), 20–26.

Spears, Larry C. (2010). Character and servant leadership: Ten characteristics of effective caring leaders. *The Journal of Virtues & Leadership, 1*(1), 25–30.

Stronge, J. H. (2002). *Qualities of effective teachers*. Alexandria, VA: ASCD.

Stronge, J. H., Richard, H. B., Catano, N. (2008). *Qualities of effective principals*. Alexandria, VA: ASCD.

Thomas, R. (2011). *You're not a real leader until you can admit to screwing up*. Retrieved May 27, 2014, from http://www.tlnt.com/2011/06/06/you're-not-a-real-leader-until-you-can-admit-to-screwing-up/.

Valdez, G. (2004, July). *Critical issue: Technology leadership: Enhancing positive educational change*. North Central Regional Educational Laboratory.

Villani, S. (2006). *Mentoring and induction programs that support new principals*. Thousand Oaks, CA: Corwin.

Wallace Foundation. (2007, October). *Education leadership: A bridge to school reform.*

Wallace Foundation. (2008, June). *Becoming a leader: Preparing school principals for today's schools.*

Wallace Foundation. (2012, January). *The school principal as leader: guiding schools to better teaching and learning. P. 6.*

Wallace Foundation. (2012, June). *The making of the principal: Five lessons in leadership training.*

Wallace Foundation. (2013). *Districts matter.*

Wright, S. P., Horn, S. P., and Sanders, W. L. (1997). Teacher and classroom context effects on student achievement: Implications for teacher evaluation. *Journal of Personnel Evaluation in Education, 11,* 57–67.

Made in the USA
Middletown, DE
06 September 2017